INSECTS AND PLANTS

INSECTS AND PLANTS

The Amazing Partnership

Elizabeth K. Cooper

Illustrated by Shirley Briggs

Harcourt, Brace & World, Inc., New York

To M. with appreciation and love

CONTENTS

I	INSECTS AND FLOWERS AT WORK	11
2	THE WORK OF A FLOWER	21
3	THE NECTAR-FEEDERS	33
4	FLOWERS AND THEIR WAYS	47
5	BEETLES AND THE FIRST FLOWERS ON THE EARTH	65
6	BEES	73
7	BEE FLOWERS	85
8	BUTTERFLIES AND MOTHS AND THE FLOWERS THEY VISIT	103
9	THE YUCCA AND ITS PARTNER	119
10	FLIES AND FLY-TRAPPING PLANTS	128
Appendixes		143
A	SOME SCIENCES OF PLANTS AND INSECTS	145
B	WHERE TO BUY LIVE SPECIMENS	147
Index		149

INSECTS AND PLANTS

1

INSECTS AND FLOWERS AT WORK

Would you like to go exploring and watch some wild creatures going about their daily business? To do this, you do not have to take a trip to Africa or to the jungles of South America. You can have exciting adventures without leaving home, or at least without going farther than the nearest field of clover, the nearest flower garden or blossoming tree. Perhaps you can do it all in your own back yard.

Start out some sunny day late in spring or during the summer. All you need to take with you are two good eyes for seeing, a nose for smelling, a tongue for tasting, ears for hearing, and fingers for feeling. A good magnifying glass is not necessary, but it will make your exploring trip more interesting.

You are going to hunt for live animals — not to catch or kill, nor even, on this first trip, to bring them back alive. You are going to hunt for some of the six-legged flying animals, the insects, that live among the flowers.

First of all, you will have to find some plants that are in bloom. Late in spring and in the summer, flowers can be found almost anywhere that green plants are growing.

Flower on tulip tree

Look for them among the weeds and grasses that grow in vacant lots and along the sides of streets and roads. Look for them in meadows and in the woods. Look for them in flower gardens and in vegetable gardens. Even in the middle of a big city, there is a good chance of finding some kinds of flowers — in public parks and squares, among the vines that grow on buildings, and in the trees along the street. Except for mosses, ferns, and evergreen trees that have cones, all of the green plants you know best have some kind of flower.

Once you find some plants in bloom, you are almost certain to find insects. Use your magnifying glass or just your eyes to look closely at any insect you may see. Find out what the insect looks like, the way it is using the different parts of its body, and what it is doing among the flowers.

Perhaps you will see a gay Monarch butterfly looping through the air and coming to light on a milkweed blossom. Notice how it holds its wings pertly upright and how it waves its delicate feelers back and forth over the flower. If you are very lucky, you may see the butterfly uncoil its long tongue from under its chin and dip it into an open blossom.

If it is near noon or early afternoon of a very hot day, you may see a fuzzy little insect hover in the air over some flowers, dart a few feet away, hover again, and finally dive into a blossom. Its black and yellow coat makes it look something like a small bee, but from its darting, hovering way of moving in the air, you can tell that it is a bee fly or hover fly.

Bee fly, or hover fly, on rose

Bumblebees and clover

If there are any bumblebees around, you cannot miss them. They make a loud bumbling noise as they wheel in the air above their favorite flowers. In early spring you can find hundreds of these bright gold-and-black fellows buzzing around every blossoming rhododendron plant. And whenever the red clover fields are in bloom, the air is filled with the sound of the bumblebees as the large, gay-colored insects go from one clover blossom to the next.

Look also for different kinds of bees — honeybees from hives and their cousins, the wild bees, that live in various kinds of nests. They are smaller than the bumblebees. Look for them around sweet-smelling flowers. Notice which flowers the bees are going to and which ones are being ignored by the bees.

Do you see any other insects around the flowers? If you look inside some of the blossoms, you may find flies, ants, or beetles crawling around. Watch them for a while and try to figure out what they are doing. Are they feeding in the flowers? Or does it seem that they have just crawled into a flower to get out of the hot sun or perhaps to seek shelter from an enemy?

You have probably noticed before this that some flowers attract more insects than others do and that certain insects seem to rush to certain kinds of flowers and pay no attention to other kinds. If you stay outside long enough on a bright, hot day, you will see that this is true. Then, if you follow with your eyes the movements of a single bee, you will discover another interesting fact. The bee goes to just *one* kind of flower. If it is visiting the blossoms of an apple tree, for instance, it goes from one apple flower to another. At the same time, a second bee may be visiting only the tiny blossoms on a vine of English ivy, and a third may be going in and out of the golden flowers on a Scotch broom plant. In Chapter Six, where you will find out more about bees, you will get some suggestions for bee-watching and for investigating their ways.

Now, take a careful look at some of the flowers that bloom around you. Make a note of the kinds you see and whether or not there are any insects in or on them. Notice the differences among the flowers, differences in size, shape, color, and kind and number of petals. Look at the flat, saucy-faced pansies of purple, brown, and yellow; at the daisies with their fringes of petals and centers of gold; at the bright yellow dandelions on their stiff, juicy stems; at blossoming fruit trees making a snowfall of dainty petals; at the bright pink and red and yellow snapdragons shaped like the jaws of animals; at pale pink and fiery red geraniums, with their little five-petal flowers grouped into large, gay flower heads; or at a horse chestnut tree with its showy spikes of creamy blooms. These are only a few of the kinds of flowers you may see where you live.

Look closely at some single flowers. You will see that some have stripes, polka dots, or centers of contrasting colors. A tiny forget-me-not has a neat yellow spot at the base of its petals. Petunias and morning-glories often have stripes like the spokes of a wheel going from the middle to the outer edge. You will find tulips of one color with blurred stripes of a second color, as though they had been painted and the paint had run. See how many different kinds of color markings you can find on flowers.

Next, bend over some of the flowers. How many kinds of scents can you smell? How different are the perfumes of roses and sweet peas from the spicy smells of stocks or carnations! Then, if you sniff a marigold, you will notice that these yellow and gold flowers have a strong and almost unpleasant odor. Smell orange blossoms, apple blossoms, or the flowers on the branch of some other kind of fruit tree. Each kind of flower, you will find, has its own special odor. Some have a faint, delicate fragrance that you cannot notice till you get very close. Some have such strong perfume that you can smell them a long way off. And some, you will find, have no fragrance at all, at least none that your human nose can detect.

Why are there so many differences among flowers? Is it just by accident that there is such variety in shape, color, pattern, and fragrance? Not at all. Flowers are the way they are because of the special job they do. A plant's flowers are given over to producing seeds just as its green leaves are given over to making food. Each part of a plant has a special job. The flower's job is to make seeds that can grow into new generations of plants. Special shapes, colors, markings, and scents all have something to do with the special work of a flower.

Flowers do not work alone. They are helped by certain insects, the "wild animals" you are watching. Insects form the largest class of animals on the earth. They can move freely from place to place, and, like all animals, they depend on plants for food. Plants, on the other hand, by using energy from sunlight, can make their own food. But they cannot move around. A rooted plant stays in one place throughout its life. What you have observed among the flowers is a working partnership between the freely moving insects and the stationary plants.

Let's think for a moment about some of the things you have seen. Observing things that happen around you is one of the scientific ways of learning. Many scientists have made great discoveries and have solved some of the

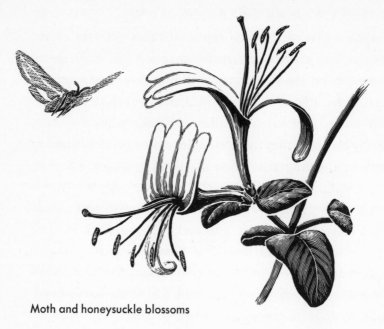

Moth and honeysuckle blossoms

mysteries of the universe by making careful observations and then thinking about the things they have observed.

You observed different kinds of flowers in bloom. You saw different kinds of insects visiting the flowers, pushing their heads or mouth parts into the blossoms. Clearly, the insects are getting something from the flowers. Probably you already know what it is. If not, here is one way to find out if you can get a honeysuckle blossom. Find one that is fresh and newly opened. Pull the flower off the vine and bite off the bottom part. Then put the end between your lips and suck on it. You will get a very sweet taste. The sweetness is from nectar, a liquid that is inside most flowers. Honeysuckles have so much nectar and it is so sweet that you can get a good taste from a single blossom. Insects that visit flowers do so to get nectar, which they use for food.

An insect is not robbing a flower when it takes its nectar, for flowers do not need the nectar they produce. The only value the nectar has to the flower is to attract nectar-feeding insects to it. As insects come to flowers to feed, they cause something important to happen. It is so important that there would be very few flowers on the earth if the insects stopped coming by. Insects assist flowers in making many good seeds that will grow into new plants. Like all good partnerships, both partners benefit from the relationship. In fact, each has become dependent on the other. Neither the nectar-feeding insects nor the plants they visit could keep going long without the other.

This amazing partnership also benefits us. We would be in a sorry state indeed if it were not for insects and flowers. We could live without bees, though we would miss their honey and their pleasant humming on a summer day. We could live without butterflies, though we would miss the sight of their bright wings flashing in the sunlight. We could live without beetles, ants, and flies and not miss them at all! Some of us could even survive without the beauty of flowers, but we would have a hard time living without the seeds they make, the fruits that grow around them, and the new generations of green plants that grow from them.

How different our earth would be! There would be

no fields of wild flowers in spring and no berries in the summer. There would be few, if any, fragrant, gaily colored flowers in our gardens. No apples, cherries, oranges, peaches, or other fruits would hang from the trees. There would be no squash, watermelons, or cucumbers, and no pumpkins for Halloween. There would be no strawberries for shortcake and no raspberries for jam. There would be no alfalfa or red clover for cattle to eat and no buckwheat for our pancakes. There would be few onions and very little cotton. We *would* have the cereal foods that come from corn, wheat, rice, oats, and other grass plants. Grasses do not depend on insect visitors to help in the making of seeds. Nearly all of the other food plants — fruits, vegetables, and nuts — depend on insects to keep them growing on the earth.

Exactly how the insects and plants work together is a strange and sometimes mysterious story. There are parts of it that still have to be discovered. This is work for scientists of the present and future who may be interested in finding out more about one of the oldest partnerships in the world. Perhaps you will be one of these scientists.

2

THE WORK OF A FLOWER

When you cut an apple, an orange, or a pear in half, you find rows of seeds. If you save the seeds and plant them, you can grow some new little trees. How did the seeds and the fruit grow from a dainty little blossom? To find out, you will need to collect some flowers and take them apart.

Take a coffee can and line it with wet paper napkins. You now have an open can that will keep your flower samples fresh while you collect them. Go outside and pick blossoms from different kinds of plants. Pick only one of a kind. Try to find one or two large ones, a tulip, lily, iris, or daffodil. Get some middle-sized ones like a pansy, snapdragon, honeysuckle, azalea, monkey flower, nasturtium, geranium, or columbine. Then collect some of the tiny flowers: forget-me-not, violet, buttercup, wild mustard, clover, or a blossom from a fruit tree, berry bush, or ivy vine. These are only suggestions. Look among the trees, weeds, and bushes and in the gardens where you live. (Be sure NOT to pick any flowers in public parks. You can learn about these by looking at them, but you may not pick them.)

Flowers of many shapes and kinds

As soon as you have a number of different kinds, or specimens, in your collecting can, you are ready to do some investigating. You will need two pieces of paper, one white and one black, a magnifying glass, and a small knife or a strong, sharp pin for some cutting apart or dissecting you may want to do. If you happen to have a microscope, you will have a chance to use it.

Take your flower specimens out of the can and look carefully at each one. Probably the first thing you will notice is the pollen, the yellow dust that comes off when you touch an open flower. Shake some pollen from one flower onto the white paper and then onto the black. Notice the color. Try this with pollen from different flowers. You will see that pollen differs in color from flower to flower. It may be pale, pale yellow, almost white. Or it may be bright yellow or a deep, golden orange. There are even a few flowers that have blue or blue-black pollen, but most of the flowers we know best have pollen in shades of yellow or orange.

Feel the pollen with your fingers. It feels very soft and somewhat sticky. Look at it through your magnify-

Flowers of many shapes and kinds

ing glass. You will be looking at grains of pollen, but through an ordinary hand lens you cannot see the separate grains.

Now, if you have a microscope, shake pollen from one flower onto a glass slide. Look at the slide, magnified two hundred to four hundred times. Then you can see the shape of the individual grains. Get a fresh slide for pollen from each kind of flower. You will discover that each kind of flower has its own kind of pollen. For instance, pollen grains from a calla lily are pale yellow, smooth, and shiny. They look like little pearls. The Shasta daisy has pollen that looks quite different. The grains are tiny golden balls with points sticking out all over. They look like the cockleburs you find in weed patches in the fall. With your microscope you can see many different kinds of pollen grains from the different flowers you have collected.

After you have examined pollen for a while, look inside some flowers and find the places where the pollen grows. On most flowers, pollen is found on the tips of slender stems, called stamens. The stamens usually grow

up around the center part of a flower: Look for the
stamens in different flowers. In some, you will find stamens with tips that are heavy with pollen. In others, you
may find stamens with no pollen. The pollen may not
yet be ripe, and in this case, the pollen sacs, called anthers, will be smooth and shut. Or the anthers may be
wide open and the pollen already gone. In a rose that
has already faded and is losing its petals, the anthers
on the tips of the stamens will look like dry, empty cases,
and that is what they are. The pollen has all been shed.
On the waxen blossom from a lemon tree, the outer stamens grow together in bunches, forming a tight, protective wall around the center part of the flower. The long,
slender anthers, with their lemon-yellow pollen, stick
out like a fringe above the stamens.

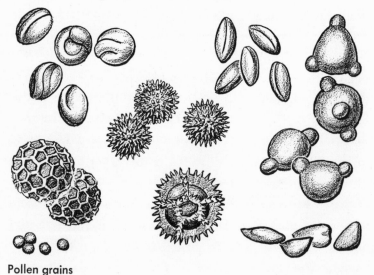

Pollen grains

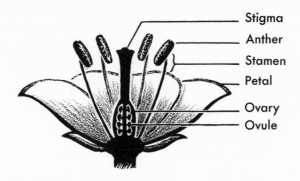

Stigma
Anther
Stamen
Petal
Ovary
Ovule

Parts of a flower

Now, take one of your largest flowers and pull off all the petals. Look at the stamens and then pull them off carefully, one by one. What you find in the very middle of the flower is the pistil. The wide part at the bottom of the pistil is the ovary, and the top of the pistil is the stigma. In many flowers, the pistil looks like a little bottle or vase.

Look at the stigma through your magnifying glass. Stigmas differ greatly in size and shape. In some flowers, the stigma is a fat little cushion, sticky and rough. In others, it is just a moist opening to the inside of the pistil.

Now you have seen a flower's seed-making parts: stamens with pollen-bearing anthers at the tips, and a pistil with an ovary at the base and a stigma at the top. Look inside some of the different flowers you have collected. In each, find the seed-making parts. Look for differences in size, shape, color, and arrangement of stamens and pistils. Use your glass to look inside some of the tiny flowers. You will be amazed at the beauty and perfection

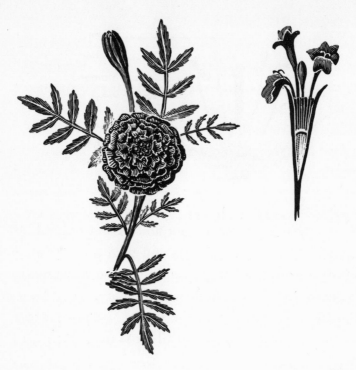

Marigold

of form you find in some of the tiniest blossoms. For instance, look at the flower head of the weedlike candytuft. It is made up of dozens of exquisite little flowers, each with four waxen petals around six green stamens tipped with golden pollen. Inside the ring of stamens is a short, wide pistil. A more beautiful flower would be hard to find.

If you take apart a marigold flower, you will find a different arrangement. What we call the flower of the marigold is really, as you can see, a whole bouquet of flowers! The center of the blossom is made up of dozens of separate little flowers, or florets, each with its own tiny petals and its own seed-making parts. All of the florets are bunched together and edged with a fringe of larger petals. You will find the same little bunches of florets when you look inside the fuzzy, purplish blossoms of red clover or a golden dandelion. Such flowers are called composites because they are composed of many small flowers together in a cluster. Daisies, asters, and sunflowers are also composites. If you take a sunflower apart, you can see the very tiny flowers in the central disc and the large yellow ray flowers around the edge.

Use your magnifying glass to look at the stigma in a geranium flower. You will see that it is split open, with delicate rays like a star. Look into a tiny blossom of wild mustard. There you will find a short, cushion-topped pistil surrounded by four purple-tipped stamens. Look inside the flowers of purple sage, of heather, and of some of the herbs that grow in gardens. When you magnify these tiny flowers, you will find that they are perfectly formed and as beautiful as the most expensive orchids in the florist's shop.

After you have taken many flowers apart and have become familiar with their stamens and pistils, put one large pistil on a piece of heavy paper. With your knife or strong pin, split open the ovary. Inside, you will find rows or clusters of pale egg-shaped things that look like unripe seeds. These are the ovules. They will grow into seeds. But first, something has to happen to them. They must be fertilized. This happens when the flower is pollinated. There are several steps to the important process of pollination.

First, pollen from an anther reaches the sticky stigma. When a grain of pollen touches the stigma, it is held fast. The moisture on the stigma makes the pollen change. A very thin tube grows out from the pollen grain and into the pistil. It grows down the pistil and into the ovary. Then it grows right into one of the little ovules. This makes an avenue from the pollen grain to the inside of the ovule. The next thing that happens is that material from the pollen grain moves down the pollen-tube avenue and into the ovule. This fertilizes the ovule.

If you have a microscope, you can do an interesting investigation. Dissolve one teaspoonful of sugar in one pint (two cupfuls) of water. Shake some pollen onto a clean glass slide and cover it with a few drops of the sugar solution. Watch through your microscope as pollen tubes grow out from the grains of pollen. Repeat the investigation with pollen from different kinds of flowers. The transparent pollen tubes you see on your slide are the same as those that go down the pistil and into an ovule.

An ovule can be fertilized by pollen from the same flower or by pollen from another flower of the same kind. When both ovule and pollen are from the same flower, the process is called self-pollination. Beans, peas, and some of the grasses seem to thrive on self-pollination, but most plants do not. For them, the seeds from self-pollination are few and poor in quality. In time, a plant that is always self-pollinated is likely to die out. Many flowers have tricky ways of preventing their pollen from reaching their own stigmas. They depend on cross-pollination. This occurs when pollen from one plant reaches the stigma in a flower of another plant of the same kind.

As soon as pollination takes place and the ovules are fertilized, they begin to grow into seeds. As the seeds ripen, the whole flower changes. The petals fade, shrivel, dry, and fall off. The ovary becomes larger and larger to hold the growing seeds. In some cases, the ovary becomes a pulpy, juicy fruit with the seeds inside.

Look inside some of these fruits: cherry, avocado, cucumber, melon, plum, grapefruit. Look for the blossom end of each. This is the place where the petals fell off as the ovary began to change into the fruit. You will also see the stem end of each fruit — the end that was fastened to the plant.

On some plants, the ripening seed pods form the hard cases we call nuts. Walnuts, almonds, chestnuts, pecans, and filberts, among others, are the fruits of trees. The parts we eat are the seeds. The inner and outer shells are parts of the seed pods.

Look for the fruits of different plants. On a rose bush, for instance, look for the plump little balls called rose hips. The ovary of a rose turns into a hip when the seeds

Flower, hips, and seeds of a wild rose

in it are ripe. If you cut one open, you will find the tiny rose seeds. Look inside different kinds of fruits and find the ripening seeds.

A fruit can grow, remember, only after the flower has been pollinated. The easiest way for this to happen is for the ripe pollen to fall onto a waiting stigma or for the pollen to be carried from stamen to stigma by the wind. Grass flowers are pollinated in these ways. The wind flowers, as they are sometimes called, are usually small and dull looking. They have no showy petals, bright colors, or sweet perfume.

Find some of the greenish-brown flowers that grow on the ends of wild grasses. Look at one through your glass and see the tiny, tiny parts. Shake a grass flower over a piece of dark paper and examine the fine, dusty pollen. Feel it with your fingers. You will find that it is not sticky like the pollen of other flowers you have been looking at. Blow some of it with your breath. See how easily the pollen moves through the air. Even a soft breeze can blow it from flower to flower. Plants that are pollinated by the wind have large amounts of very fine, dry, light pollen. They must produce a great deal of pollen because so much of it is wasted as it is blown about. Only a small amount ever falls on the tiny stigmas where it can be used to make seeds. Most of it falls on the ground, on water, or is blown up into the atmosphere, where it stays till rain, snow, or a downward movement of air brings it back to the earth. What a waste of pollen!

It is a different story for the pollen of violets, squash flowers, clover, roses, and thousands of other kinds of flowers that are not pollinated by wind. They have ways of making a small amount of pollen do the work that must be done if seeds are to grow. They get their pollen from stamen to stigma by a kind of airmail, special delivery. They use the services of insects! Insects pick up pollen from ripe stamens and deliver it to the place where it can do the most good — the stigma.

Flowers have different ways of offering their nectar to their insect visitors. There are different ways, too, in which the insects may become aware that nectar is there, ready for them. Showy petals, bright colors, lines and dots to mark the way, and odors that appeal to the insects all help carry the message: "Nectar is ready! Come and get it!" The insects get the message, fly to the waiting flowers, and begin to feed. While feeding or while dipping in and out of flowers, the insects do the job of pollination. They are not, of course, deliberately serving the flowers. From the insect's point of view, all it is doing is gathering nectar, the food it needs to keep alive.

THE NECTAR-FEEDERS

There are hundreds of thousands of kinds of insects on the earth today. There are only a few kinds, however, that pollinate flowers. They are the ones that have mouth parts for lapping or sucking up nectar and hairy bodies on which pollen collects when the insects dip into the flowers. They also have ways of finding flowers and wings that carry them quickly from one flower to the next.

Just think what would happen if all insects had to walk! Watch an ant crawl up the stem of a flower. It seems to be racing along on its six sturdy legs — up the stem, around the outside of the flower, into the flower, out again, and back down the stem to the ground. Even though it runs as fast as its legs can take it, it is still a long trip for the ant to go in and out of a single flower. It is an even longer trip from one flower to another. Pollination would be a slow process, indeed, if flowers depended on walking or crawling insects to do the job. A flying insect can make the trip from flower to flower with a quick flash of wings and without losing any of the precious pollen.

You will want to get a good close look at some of the

insects that fly around the flowers. Some people catch and kill insects in order to study them. This is necessary for anyone who wants to study an insect for a long time or who wants to dissect it and find out about its inside parts. You are more interested right now in finding out how insects look on the outside, how they move around, and how they are able to sip nectar and gather pollen. To find out these things, you should look at live insects. Look at them as they are going about their business among the flowers, or catch them one by one and examine them in observation cages. Here is one way to do it.

Collect some empty clear plastic jars and pill bottles to use for observation cages. Use a jar or bottle that is just a little bit larger than the insect you want to observe. Catch the insect right in the observation cage, or catch it in a net and then put it into the plastic cage and put on the lid. There will be enough air inside for the short time you need to keep the insect captive. Once the insect is closed inside the jar, use your magnifying glass to look at it. By turning the observation cage, you can get a good look at your specimen from all sides. When you are through looking at a captured insect, open the cage and let it go about its business.

When you catch a flower-visiting insect, look first at its body. You will see that it has three parts. There is the front part, the head; the middle part, the thorax; and the tail part, the abdomen. The word, insect, comes from the Latin word, *insectum,* which means "cut into" or "divided into." All insects have bodies that are divided into three parts. Most of the flower visitors have bodies that are covered with hair. Look at the body of a moth or a butterfly or a bee. On some you will see hair so thick and long that it looks like fur. Most flies are less furry but have long, sharp-looking hairs growing out of their bodies. When a hairy insect brushes against a clump of pollen inside a flower, it cannot avoid picking up a load of the sticky grains.

Look at the legs of the insects you catch. Count them. You will find that there are six, unless your specimen lost one in a fight or accident, which sometimes happens. Nearly all insects, when they are adults, have three pairs of legs. Watch for ways in which some insects use their legs to comb their hair, clean their feelers, and wipe their faces.

Look carefully at the feelers, or antennae, that grow out of the heads. These are usually slender jointed parts that move in all directions. On butterflies, the antennae are likely to have little knobs or clubs on the tips. The antennae of moths are often like two large feathers sticking out of their heads like plumes on a lady's hat.

When you look at the head of one of your insects, you will discover that a large part of it is taken up by the eyes. Most insects have two very large eyes and two or more tiny ones. The large ones are the compound eyes, which are made up of many, many separate lenses. When an insect looks around, each little lens sees part of the

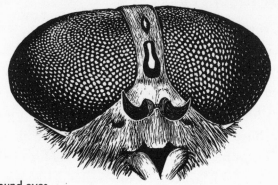

Compound eyes

scene. All of the lenses together give the insect a general picture of its surroundings. The small eyes are called simple eyes. They see only light and dark and seem to help the insect to react to what it sees with its compound eyes.

As you look at these complicated little animals and see how they wave their antennae, move their heads, walk with their dainty legs, and fly with their wings, you may wonder about their brains. How intelligent is an insect? Scientists tell us that, instead of a brain, an insect has a mass of nerve cells. Insects cannot really think. They do not have intelligence, at least not the kind of intelligence we find in people. However, insects have marvelous powers that enable them to do many things that we, with our intelligence, cannot do. We do not really understand just how some insects are able to do all the things they do. Some kinds, especially the bees, are described as being "clever."

There are other insects, such as some members of the

fly family, that seem to be "stupid." They are easily lost, tricked, and put off the track. You will read in some books about the "clever bees" and the "stupid flies," but it is probably wrong to call insects either clever or stupid. The insects do the things they do because it is their nature to do so. Their actions are guided by their mysterious built-in instincts. They are born with the ability to do the things they need to do in order to survive.

In many of their actions, insects are led by their senses. They seem to have the same senses we have — sight, hearing, taste, smell, and touch — plus others that we do not have. Some insects, for instance, can sense changes in temperature and humidity of the air. Others seem to be guided by a kind of radar system of their own. Insects are especially good at seeing things move. They can also see some colors and can tell one color from another. This is especially true for butterflies, bees, and the other nectar-feeders. Some can see certain colors more easily than others. They show this by visiting the flowers of the colors they see best.

A few kinds of insects are thought to be deaf. Others seem able to hear sounds beyond those that we can hear. Yet they have no ears. At least, they have no parts that we would call ears. Some of them hear with their antennae. Some hear with other parts of their bodies. We say that insects can hear. Yet they probably no not hear the things we hear. They hear the things that are important to them — the approach of another insect that can be

pounced upon and eaten; warning sounds to tell them
an enemy is near; sounds of small movements that lead
an insect to its mate. To an insect, the air may be filled
with thousands of tiny sounds that they can hear but we
cannot.

With their mouth parts, some insects can taste sweet,
sour, bitter, and salt. Wasps and ants seem to do this with
their antennae, which must be very handy for them. If
they don't like the taste of something, they can keep a
feeler's length way from it. Butterflies and honeybees
have an even more special way of tasting something. All
they have to do is to step on it! They can taste things
with their feet!

Most insects have a highly developed sense of smell.
They have no noses, and yet they can smell. They smell,
as far as we can tell, with their antennae. Some moths can
locate their mates more than a mile away and fly straight
to them just by using their sense of smell.

Just think what some insects can do with their two
antennae! They can hear, taste, and smell with them.
They can also use them as kinds of thermometers and
barometers. Antennae seem to register differences in
temperature and other conditions of the air. And, of
course, the antennae, or feelers, are also used to feel
with. Antennae are indeed useful things to have growing
out of the top of one's head — if one is an insect!

Since insects have no noses, you may wonder how they
breathe. No, they do not do *this* with their antennae.

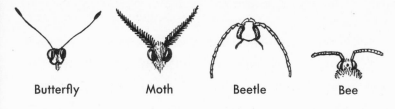

| Butterfly | Moth | Beetle | Bee |

Antennae

They get air through a row of little holes in the sides of their bodies. The holes are called spiracles. An insect breathes in and out through its spiracles, using air as we do to keep alive. You could hold a moth's head under water for hours without harming the insect. But don't try to hold its body under water. Even with its head sticking out, the moth would die in time from lack of oxygen.

If you have been watching and catching insects among the flowers, you have probably discovered some of the different kinds that feed on nectar — bees, beetles, wasps, flies, butterflies, and moths. They all visit flowers, sip nectar in one way or another, and carry pollen. And they all have wings.

Different kinds of insects have different kinds of wings — heavy wings, delicate, transparent ones, or wings covered with colorful scales. Some have four wings, some two, and some have no wings at all. According to the number and kind of wings, all insects are classified in groups, called orders. Each order has a name that tells something about the wings of the insects in that group. The names were made from Greek words. Most of them end in "ptera," from the Greek word for wing. The first

part of each name tells the kind of wings. The order
Homoptera, for instance, includes insects whose four
wings are all alike. *Homo* means "equal" or "the same"
in Greek. Homoptera, then, means equal wings or wings
that are all the same.

Of all the orders of insects, only four include typical
nectar-feeders. Here are the four orders and the kinds
of insects in each that have mouth parts and feeding
habits that lead them to flowers.

ORDER COLEOPTERA. These are the beetles. There are
more species, or kinds, of beetles than of any other insects in the world. Beetles are also the oldest of the nectar-
feeders. That is, they have been on the earth longer than
any of the others.

Coleoptera means "sheath wing." Beetles have two
pairs of wings. The front wings are stiff and hard. The
soft rear ones are used for flying. When a beetle is not
flying, its hard wings close over its flying ones, forming a
protective cover, or sheath. The next time you see a
ladybug or another kind of beetle, look at the way its
hard wings close over its flying ones.

Catch some kind of beetle and examine it in your observation cage. The American stag beetle, which you
may call a pinching bug, is easy to pick up. Notice its
jaws. The jaws of beetles are amazing. They can cut,
bite, tear, chew, or suck. Some, like those of the stag
beetle, are huge and lined with sharp teeth. Their
tongues, with which they can suck or lap up nectar, are

Flying wings fold under sheath wings

Beetle wings

short. They can reach nectar only in flowers that are fairly flat and wide open.

Beetles feed on leaves, stems, roots, fruits, and other plant parts. For refreshment, they seem to enjoy stopping in at a flower for a sip of nectar. Sometimes a beetle will also help itself to bites of petals or stamens or to a mouthful of pollen. Since beetles feed on so many kinds of things, they are not dependent on nectar for their food.

ORDER DIPTERA. These are the flies. Diptera means "two wings." Most flies, like the common housefly, have only a single pair of wings. Some flies rarely visit flowers, while others are constant nectar-feeders. The flies with short tongues can reach only the nectar that is out in the open. They sometimes crawl around in flowers and seem to be looking for nectar but are unable to find it unless it is exposed. There are flowers that have developed ways of tricking such flies — leading them in, holding them prisoner, and even, in some cases, killing them. The short-tongued flies have a varied diet and do not depend on nectar for food.

The story is different for the flies with the long tongues. They can dip into flowers and sip nectar easily. The drone fly and the hover fly (sometimes called bee fly) are true nectar-feeders. They have no way of getting food except by sipping nectar.

Flies are often easy to catch in a jar. Catch and examine the short-tongued housefly. Then try to find one of the long-tongued hover flies. It has a hairy black-and-yellow coat like that of a bee, and it hovers over flowers.

ORDER HYMENOPTERA. This order includes the bees, wasps, sawflies, and ants. Many of them, especially the bees and wasps, are constant flower visitors. Most of them, including some ants in certain stages, have clear, shiny wings that looks like cellophane. Hymenoptera means "membrane wing." A membrane is a thin layer of skin.

Bees are the most important insects in the order Hymenoptera. They are also the most important of all the flower pollinators. They feed on only two things—nectar and pollen. They have long tongues for sucking up nectar and chewing mouth parts, which they use on pollen. Beetles, as you know, feed on a bit of pollen from time to time, but only the bees depend on pollen, as well as on nectar, for food.

Many bees have stingers. If you want to take a close

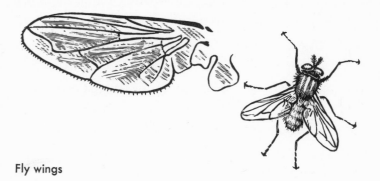

Fly wings

look at a bee, you will have to be careful not to get stung. Bees are gentle insects and will not sting unless they are injured. Since you cannot always tell exactly what might injure a bee, it is a good idea NOT to touch one. Do not even touch one that you think is dead. It may merely be stunned. When it comes to, it may give you a painful sting. There are ways, however, of catching bees. Put a few drops of honey or perfume on the inside of the lid to a plastic jar. Lay the lid, top down, near a place where you

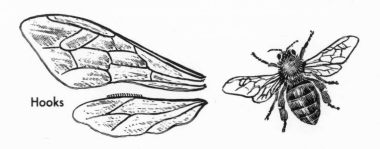

Hooks

Bee wings

have seen bees gathering. This may be near a flowering
bush or tree or beside a dripping faucet, where bees have
been coming for water. Wait quietly. As soon as you see
a bee or two on the lid, creep up softly and fit the jar
down on top of the lid. With your bee inside the transparent jar, you can safely examine it from all sides. Try
to get a good look at several bees before you read about
bees in Chapter Six.

Wasps are also nectar-feeders, but they make only a
few flower stops compared with those of the bees. A wasp
takes only the nectar it needs at the time and then flies
off. It does not store nectar for the winter or collect nectar and pollen to feed the young as bees do. Yet wasps
are useful to many plants, and there are some that would
soon die out if wasps stopped visiting. In the story of
the wasp and the fig tree on page 58, you will read about
a little wasp in a very special kind of partnership with a
plant.

If you live where there are wasps, put a few drops of
honey or orange marmalade outside on a window sill.
You may be able to lure the wasps there to feed. Do not
try to catch any. Some wasps are gentle and harmless, but
the members of the hornet family have stings that can
hurt a great deal. It is best to watch them from a distance
or through a window or screen.

ORDER LEPIDOPTERA. These are the moths and butterflies. Lepidoptera means "scale wing." When you touch
the wings of one of these insects, you get a kind of soft,

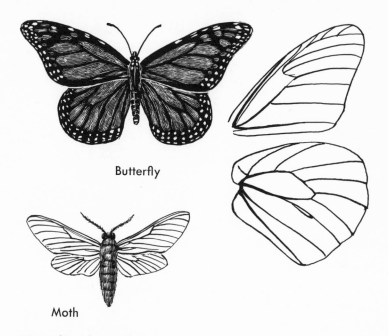

Butterfly

Moth

Wings of Lepidoptera insects

powdery dust on your fingers. The dust is made up of tiny, tiny scales of many colors. When you find a dead butterfly or moth, scrape all of the scales off one of the wings. Examine the scales through a hand lens. Then examine the wing from which the scales were removed. You will see that it is a clear, colorless membrane. The scales give the wings of these insects their colors and patterns. If you have a microscope, you will enjoy looking at the scales you have scraped off. You will see that the scales have interesting shapes as well as colors.

Moths and butterflies are very important nectar-feeders. Their mouths are good for nothing but nectar. Their tongues are as long as the tongues of bees and, in some cases, much longer. Some of the hawk moths, or sphinx moths, have tongues more than three inches long. There are moths that live in the jungles that have tongues nearly a foot long! A moth or butterfly keeps its tongue coiled up under its chin when it is not in use. Then, when the insect comes to a flower, it uncoils its tongue, dips it into the blossom, and sucks up nectar as you drink soda pop through a straw. Butterflies and moths are completely dependent on nectar for their food. They do not store up any nectar and so can live only where flowers are in bloom.

These insects are not hard to catch. Use a big observation cage for each one you catch. Do not keep it long, for it may harm its delicate wings by beating them against the sides of the jar. If you can, put a sweet-smelling flower in with the insect. It may show you how it uses its legs, wings, antennae, and even its unusual coiled-up tongue. Look at everything carefully through your hand lens and then set the insect free.

Chapter

4

FLOWERS AND THEIR WAYS

When you look at a large, bright-colored flower and smell its sweet perfume, you are not surprised to see a bee making a beeline to its center. You can tell that the flower has drawn the insect to it. You know that the bee will find nectar in the flower and will help the flower by pollinating it. It all works out so neatly that it seems as though the flower and the bee *know* what they are doing.

This, of course, is not so. The bee is merely using its food-gathering instincts, following clues from its senses of sight, smell, and taste to the nectar and pollen. When we watch the wonderful partnership between plants and insects, we must always be careful to remember that neither plants nor insects are like people. Otherwise, we may become falsely romantic and think that flowers knowingly dress themselves in lovely colors and make themselves sweet with perfume to charm the insects and lure them in; and that bees are using intelligence when they fly directly to the nectar in a sweet-smelling flower. Such a story may be charming, but the truth is really more wonderful.

All living things reproduce. That is, they make more

of their own kind. Plants, like animals, resemble their parents. Even though a new generation of plants is like the plants that produced it, there are small differences among the offspring. There may be some with larger, more colorful flowers. There may be some with more nectar or with stronger fragrance. The larger, brighter, sweeter flowers attract more insects. They are sure to be pollinated and to form many good seeds. From their seeds, more plants with showy, sweet flowers will grow. Again, those that are most attractive to insects will have the best chance of being pollinated and will form the most and the best seeds. And so it goes, over and over again.

This has been going on for millions of years and is still going on. When you look at flowers today, you can see the results. Flowers that depend on insects to pollinate them have special colors and other features that attract insect visitors.

Insects, too, have changed over the years. The nectar-feeders whose mouth parts are best for sipping nectar have the best chance to get food and to live long enough to reproduce their own kind. The young, being very like their parents, will also have good mouths for sipping nectar from flowers. Generation after generation, the nectar-feeders best able to get the nectar are the ones that survive.

This process of change and survival was first explained more than a hundred years ago by a scientist named Charles Darwin. He studied many kinds of plants and animals in different parts of the world. He wondered about many things he saw. Why are there so many kinds of living things? Why are there so many differences among them? Why do some kinds die out or become extinct, while others live on for millions of years? He had a theory about all this. We can explain his theory in four steps.

1. All living things have many offspring. Each generation produces far more young plants and animals than could possibly live on the earth. The environment cannot support all of them.

2. There is a struggle for survival. The living things that are best fitted to the environment survive. They thrive and make more of their own kind. Those not fitted to the environment gradually die out.

3. The kinds of plants and animals with the best ways of getting what they need from the environment are the ones that survive. Those that are less successful in getting the things they need are the kinds that do not live to reproduce.

4. Those that survive (plants and animals) pass on their characteristics to the next generation.

This process of selection and survival is repeated over and over again. In each generation, the plants and animals that have ways of getting what they need in the places where they grow will live and reproduce. Insects that have mouth parts for getting food from flowers will

live on — as long as there are flowers where they live.
Likewise, plants that have ways of getting insects to pollinate them will live on — as long as there are insects
nearby. Plants and insects have come to depend upon
each other during the millions and millions of years they
have been on the earth. They have both changed in ways
that make them fit together. They have become adapted
to each other.

Plants that depend on insects have developed some interesting features. They have to attract insects from a
distance, help them spot a single blossom among many,
and then lead the insect right into the flower where it
cannot help touching the seed-making parts.

The odor of a flower probably draws the insect first.
Nectar-feeders can smell better than they can see. From
far off, they catch a flower's scent and follow it. When an
insect gets near the flower, it sees the color of the petals
and usually flies to the edge of the blossom. From there
on, it makes its way to the nectar that is inside.

There may be an especially strong perfume coming
from the center of the flower. The insect can follow the
scent trail to the nectar, which has no scent of its own.
In many flowers, the insect follows a pattern of dots,
lines, or color spots that lead it to the nectar. Such patterns are called nectar guides.

Go on a flower hunt and look for nectar guides in
flowers like the following:

Nectar guides on a day lily

DAFFODIL. There may be a cup of bright yellow against paler yellow petals. Sometimes there are fine lines of deeper color leading from the edge of the cup to the center.

NARCISSUS. Usually a yellow center leads the insect in by scent as well as by color. The odor of the center is stronger than that of the rest of the blossom.

NASTURTIUM. Here you will find darker lines and patches on yellow and orange petals.

GARDEN PRIMROSE (PRIMULA). Look for the lovely flower-shaped centers, usually yellow or some light color, against blue, purple, or magenta.

SWEET WILLIAM. Each little flower has rings or spots around the middle, sometimes white against a color or a deep color against a lighter one.

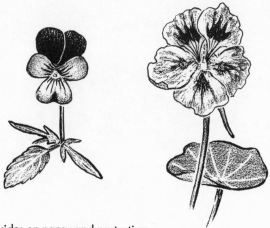

Nectar guides on pansy and nasturtium

GERANIUM. There are many kinds of nectar guides among the geraniums. Some flowers have delicate stripes leading to the center. On Martha Washington geraniums (pelargoniums), you will find many spots and stripes to guide the insects.

TIGER LILY. This and the common day lilies have brown spots and broken lines leading to the nectar.

MONKEY FLOWER (MIMULUS). Here you find a series of spots and dots like footprints for the insects to follow.

PANSY. This little flower often has lines, spots, and a contrasting center to guide insects to the tiny seed-making parts. In fact, pansies often have nectar guides on top of nectar guides. A visiting insect could hardly lose its way in a pansy!

Look inside some of the following flowers and find their nectar guides:

rhododendron	forget-me-not	horse chestnut
azalea	Scotch broom	violet
Virginia bluebell	cowslip	morning-glory
butter-and-eggs	iris	poppy
foxglove	orchid	amaryllis
hollyhock	delphinium	bindweed

These are only a few suggestions to start you looking. You will find nectar guides in many flowers other than those listed above. You will also see many flowers with no nectar guides at all. Sometimes there are two flowers on the same plant, and only one will have nectar guides. We might guess that the one with the guides will be more successful in leading insects in. On the other hand, it is possible that insects visiting that kind of flower can find their way in an occasional flower that does not have guides. They may have been trained by the guides in the other flowers of the same kind. There is so much variety in nature, and there are so many exceptions to every rule! Many mysteries are still to be solved.

In general, the kinds of flowers that have nectar guides are the ones in which the nectar is deeply hidden. Flowers that hold their nectar in the open do not need guides. The place where nectar is produced is called the nectary. Your tongue found the nectary at the base of a honeysuckle flower. In flowers of the iris family and in many lilies, the nectary is at the base of the pistil. Such flowers often have so much nectar that the bottom part of the

Nectar spurs on columbine and nasturtium

blossom is filled with it. A buttercup has unusual nectaries. Pick some buttercups, pull off the petals carefully, and look at them through your magnifying glass. Look for the tiny flap at the base of each petal. It is called a nectar scale. It holds the flower's nectary.

Honeysuckles and flowers of the trumpet vine have their nectaries at the bottom of such long tubes that only the insects with very long tongues (or hummingbirds) can ever reach the nectar. Some flowers have their nectaries in special spurs. You can see the nectar spurs on nasturtiums, red valerians, columbines, and on some violets and some kinds of orchids. Insects have to work hard and follow guides to reach the nectar that collects in one of those long spurs.

In the wild geranium, forget-me-not, and in many other wide-open flowers, the tiny drops of nectar are lightly screened by a few soft hairs. It is believed that the hairs inside the flowers keep out dew and rain, which would dilute or weaken the sweetness of the nectar. Look for flower hairs in the specimens you examine.

When an insect goes into a flower for nectar, it may shake pollen from stamen to stigma of the same flower. When it goes to the next flower, it carries with it some pollen from the first one. Thus, an insect can cause both self- and cross-pollination. Some flowers, however, protect themselves from self-pollination. One way in which this is done is by having stamens and pistils ripen at different times.

In geraniums, the pistil ripens before the stamens do. When a pistil is ready to receive pollen, the pollen has to come from an older flower. In the figwort flower, it is just the opposite. The stamens ripen first. When pollen is ripe in a figwort blossom, its own pistil is not yet ready to receive it. By the time its pistil is ready, its own pollen is gone. It must then get pollen from a younger flower.

In the garden plant, red valerian (also called Jupiter's-beard), the stamens ripen first and the pistil soon after. When an insect comes to the flower, it gets a load of pollen from the ripe stamens. It cannot pollinate the flower, for the stigma is not yet sticky and ready for it. In another flower of the same kind, the stigma may be ready and waiting. By now, the stamens, which may still be loaded with pollen, have moved out of the way. The visiting bee bumps into the stigma without touching the stamens. In this way, the plant is almost certain not to be self-pollinated.

Some primroses grow two types of flowers. One type has long stamens and short pistils. The other has long pistils and short stamens. This arrangement makes it difficult for pollen to reach the pistil in the same flower.

Blossoms of the salvia family have most unusual ways of preventing self-pollination. Salvias are true sages. Look for at least one of the kinds listed below:

Salvias in herb gardens:
  dark purple-blue sage (blue meadow sage)
  yellow-flowered sage
  pale purple-flowered sage
Salvias in flower gardens:
  scarlet salvia
Salvias of Western prairies and mountains:
  blue sage

All of these salvias (or sages) have special ways of making certain that visiting bees, which are very fond of their nectar and pollen, cross-pollinate their flowers and avoid self-pollination. The blue meadow sage has perhaps the best system of them all. When the flowers are young, the stamens are curved and attached with a kind of hinge to the bottom of the pistil. The stigma sticks out above and away from the stamens. When a bee enters the flower, it pushes against the bottom of the hinged ends of the stamens. Down come the stamens, dusting the bee's back with pollen and shutting the bee off from the stigma. The bee gets its sip of nectar and then flies off without ever touching the stigma. Later, when the

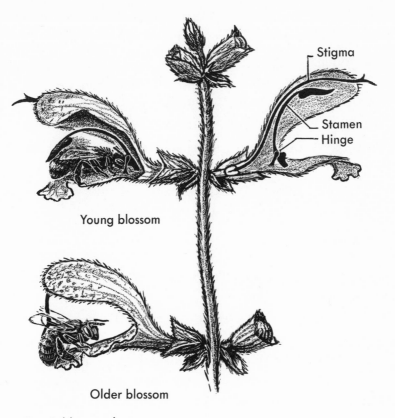

Stigma

Stamen
Hinge

Young blossom

Older blossom

Bees in blue meadow sage

bee visits an older blossom, it bumps right into the stigma. In the older flowers, the pistils hang down in such a way that the bee cannot avoid leaving some pollen from its back on the sticky stigma.

An extreme way of preventing self-pollination, and probably one of the oldest ways, is for pistils and stamens to grow on separate flowers but on the same plant. You can see this arrangement on the vines that produce cucumbers, squash, watermelons, pumpkins, and gourds. Each vine has two kinds of flowers. One kind has stamens but no pistils. These are the male flowers. They produce the pollen. The other flowers, the females, have pistils but no stamens. They produce the ovules, which develop into seeds after they have received pollen from the male flowers. The fruits, which are fleshy coverings for the seeds, grow from only the female blossoms. You have often seen the seeds inside watermelon, cucumber, squash, and pumpkin fruits. The male flowers simply wither and fall off the vines after their pollen has been shed.

Mulberry trees, beech trees, and a number of other plants also have separate male and female flowers growing on the same plant.

Some fig trees are even more extreme. There are wild trees that have male and female flowers but produce no edible fruits. The trees that produce the figs we eat have only female flowers. For such trees, self-pollination is obviously impossible. The pollen has to come from another

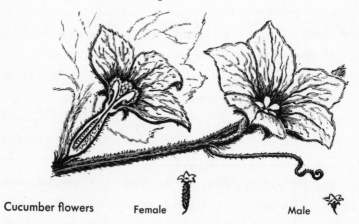

Cucumber flowers   Female   Male

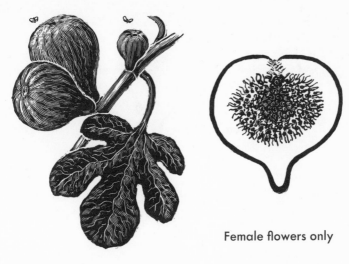

Female flowers only

Ripe Smyrna figs

kind of fig tree, one on which male flowers grow.

Since ancient times, the wild caprifig (meaning "goat fig") has supplied the pollen, which has been delivered from male to female flower by a small wasp, the Blastophaga. Only with the help of this particular insect can fig trees produce edible fruits. The pollen cannot be transferred by wind or carried by another kind of insect.

To find out why this is so, look inside a ripe Smyrna fig. Cut one open crosswise and another lengthwise. Study the inside parts. Bite into a fig and taste the juicy sweetness and crunch the tiny seeds with your teeth. It may seem to you that the fig is like many other fruits, a sweet, fleshy lobe that has grown around its ripening seeds. In most ways, however, a fig is *not* like other fruits. It is sometimes called "a fruit without a flower."

The truth is that fig flowers grow *inside the fruit!*

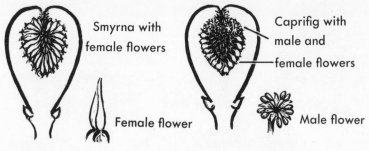

Smyrna with female flowers

Caprifig with male and female flowers

Female flower

Male flower

Unripe figs

That is, they grow inside the part we call the fruit, which is really a hollow container that holds first the flowers and then the fruits. The true fig fruits are the fleshy bits that cover the hard, gritty seeds.

If you study the inside of a ripe fig or the picture of one, you can see how the flowers are arranged — flowers without petals, flowers shut up inside a tough green bag. No passing bee or darting butterfly can stop by for a sip and leave behind the needed grains of pollen. How, then, are the fig flowers pollinated?

If you have a chance to visit a Smyrna fig tree, look at an unripe fig. You will find a very small opening in the green covering. Through this tiny entrance, pollen will be delivered to the female flowers inside. A Blastophaga wasp, which is small enough to pass through the opening, will make the delivery. After the flowers have been pollinated, the hole will grow shut.

Most of the figs we eat, including the Smyrna, come from plants that grew originally in the warm lands around the Aegean and Mediterranean Seas. There the fig trees and the Blastophaga wasps began their partnership.

They have been in business for thousands of years that we know about, and perhaps for millions of years before men were around to keep records. At any rate, the ancient Greeks, who had orchards of fruit-producing fig trees, always saw to it that there were some wild caprifigs growing nearby. The caprifig trees, with their hard, inedible fruits, are still needed for the fig-wasp partnership.

In the early spring, the Blastophaga lays eggs inside one of the figs on a caprifig tree. These figs contain both male and female flowers. The wasp crawls to the far end of the fig, where the female flowers grow. There the eggs are deposited. Galls then form around the tiny eggs. Galls are swellings or growths on plants caused by some kind of irritation. In this case, the plant is irritated by the presence of the eggs, and so a small gall grows around each egg. The galls serve as incubators for the eggs, which soon hatch into larvae, then become pupae, and finally adults, each inside its own little gall.

By early summer, the larvae have all become adult

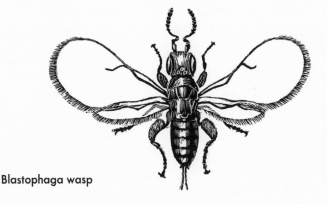

Blastophaga wasp

insects. There are females with wings and wingless males. A male wasp chews a hole in its gall prison and then looks around for a female. When it finds one, it chews a hole in the female's gall and the wasps mate. After mating, the female makes the gall hole larger and crawls out of the gall, leaving the male behind to die. All of this, remember, takes place inside the fig that grows on a wild fig tree. Male Blastophaga wasps never get out. They hatch inside the fig, go through larva and pupa stage, become adults, mate, and die, all while imprisoned in the fig.

The female, however, has a different kind of life. After mating, it makes its way to the opening at the end of the fig. In doing this, it has to crawl over the male flowers that grow near the fig's entrance. It picks up a load of pollen as its body brushes against the stamens of the male flowers.

Once free of the fig, the female spreads its wings and travels by air. If Smyrna trees or other fig trees with female flowers are growing nearby, the wasp finds its way to one of the figs. It crawls in through the opening at the end of the fig, walks around among the flowers, and tries to find a place to settle down and lay some eggs. It is unable to do this because of the very tall pistils in the flowers. It cannot find a comfortable place to stop for its egg-laying. Nevertheless, the Blastophaga seems to keep looking and trying, and as it moves among the flowers, it dusts them with pollen from the caprifig. For some mysterious reason, the wasp goes from one fig to another, searching in vain for a suitable fig in which to deposit eggs and, of course, pollinating the flowers as it goes. A single little female wasp can take care of many fig flowers.

The edible figs, which have been pollinated by the wasp's futile attempts to lay eggs, now grow shut. Seeds form and ripen, and the figs become sweet and juicy. We then pick them and eat them fresh, or we can dry them.

Meanwhile, the little wasp has given up trying to lay its eggs in the edible figs. It makes its way to a fig that will produce not sweet, juicy fruits, but galls that will serve as incubators for the eggs. Gall figs, as you know, grow on caprifig trees. A special kind of gall fig also grows, late in the fall, on the upper branches of certain other kinds of fig trees. Such gall figs serve only as incubators for the wasps and as shelters for them during the winter. They do not supply pollen, and so the caprifigs are still needed in the spring.

The ancient Greeks knew of the importance of caprifigs and so did the Romans. Sometimes the ancient fig growers grafted caprifig branches onto the trees that produced edible figs. More often, they simply tied or hung caprifig branches to their orchard fig trees. The caprifig branches, bearing their inedible figs with galls and wasps inside, made it possible for the fruit-producing fig trees to be pollinated.

In time, the importance of the fig-wasp partnership was forgotten, especially among the people of Western nations. In 1880, Smyrna fig trees were first brought to

California to begin the fig-growing industry in the United States. The trees were imported from their native lands around the Mediterranean Sea. Only Smyrnas were brought in, and these, of course, have only female flowers, though the fig growers did not know this at the time. The imported trees grew well, but the figs fell off the trees before they could form seeds or ripen. The whole thing was quite a mystery until, in 1899, some wild fig trees, caprifigs, were brought to California from the same Mediterranean lands. The caprifigs were planted near the Smyrnas. The caprifigs had galls, and the galls had Blastophaga wasps inside. The mystery was solved, and the wasps gave the fig business a start in California.

Smyrna figs are still produced by means of what is called caprification—the use of caprifigs and Blastophaga wasps. From the Smyrna fig has come the juicy white Calimyrna, which is, as the name suggests, a kind of Smyrna fig grown in California.

Today there are ways of growing good seedless figs without pollination of any kind. But the little Blastophaga is still needed for producing the best figs used for drying. Every time we eat a dried fig, we have reason to say thank you to a tiny, strange, and not very handsome wasp, the Blastophaga.

BEETLES AND THE FIRST FLOWERS ON THE EARTH

There were green plants on the earth millions of years before there were any plants with flowers. During the ages when coal was being formed, there were ferns that grew as tall as trees grow today. There were rushes, much like our little horsetails, but hundreds of times as big. There were strange-looking trees with feathery green pompons on top. There were trees that looked like giant palms and others that bore cones like those on the modern pine.

There were also many insects. Some were like nothing that lives on the earth today. Others were like modern insects but much larger. There were dragonflies nearly thirty inches across with wings outspread. There were cockroaches several times the size of their modern descendants. There were no bees, no wasps, no moths, no butterflies. There were no nectar-feeders of any kind, for there was no nectar on which they could feed.

When and how did flowers begin? This is a question that interests scientists. They have figured out some possible answers, though no one can be sure exactly what happened in those long-ago times. There were, of course,

Coal Age plants

no people on the earth when flowers appeared. People did not come till millions and millions of years after flowers and nectar-feeding insects had begun their wonderful partnership.

All we can do today is to study the records of past ages printed in the layers of rocks that we dig out of the earth. In these prints, called fossils, we see what plants and animals of the past were like. Scientists then use their knowledge of living things today in an effort to explain how plants and animals may have affected each other as they lived together millions of years ago.

We know from fossils that beetles have been on the earth for a long, long time, far longer than bees, butter-flies, or other nectar-feeding insects. Some scientists think that beetles may have had something to do with the early development of flowers. Beetles may have fed in some of the first flowers on the earth. They may have been the earliest kind of insects to use pollen or nectar for food and thus begin the insect-flower partnership that has been going on ever since.

By the end of dinosaur times, some of the flowers we know today were already developed. Magnolias opened their waxen cups, and dogwood blossomed in the spring and made light patterns among the green leaves of the forests. Shrubs and trees like laurel, sassafras, willow, fig, beech, elm, and oak were bursting with blooms.

Today, after millions of years of partnership, beetles and flowers have some strange and surprising ways of

Dogwood blossoms

fitting together. Modern beetle flowers attract their insect visitors mainly by smell. Beetles are drawn to the flowers by their spicy, fruity, or animal odors.

Since beetles feed on many kinds of things, including dead and decaying animals, some beetle flowers smell anything but sweet (except, perhaps, to a beetle!). One giant flower that grows in far-off Sumatra smells like decaying flesh, which is called carrion. This attracts the carrion beetles, which pollinate the plant.

Flower of western spicebush

In California, spicebushes grow wild along some of the streams and canyons. They have fairly large red flowers that smell like old grapes or wine. When a flower is ready to receive pollen, its outer petals open wide, but the inner petals hold together like a little pouch with an opening on the top. The strong winelike smell comes out through the opening. Little beetles, commonly known as flower beetles, are attracted by the odor and crawl into the pouch of petals. Once inside, a beetle is trapped, for the inner petals are covered with tiny hairs that point downward. The beetle cannot crawl up, and the opening at the top of the pouch of petals is too small to allow the insect to spread its wings and fly to freedom.

While the beetle is held inside the flower, it receives a good dusting of pollen. As soon as the stamens begin to release pollen, the flower's inside parts bend toward the stigma and shield it. Thus, the flower cannot be self-pollinated. When the pollen has been shed, the inner petals open, and the beetle is free to fly away, after having been held captive for one, two, or even three days.

You would think that after such an experience the beetle would avoid other spicebush flowers. It does nothing of the kind. In fact, it does just the opposite. It goes right to another flower of the same kind and down into another trap! This time, its pollen-covered body hits the stigma and leaves on it some pollen from the first flower. Then the whole process is repeated. It happens over and over again as long as the spicebushes are in bloom. These plants seem to be entirely dependent on the tiny flower beetles for pollination.

If you cannot find any of the red-flowered spicebushes near your home, you may find another shrub of the same family. This one has large chocolate-colored flowers. When you crush one of the flowers, you get a strong scent — not of chocolate, but of strawberries! For this reason,

Pond lily with beetles

the plant is commonly called a strawberry shrub. It is also known as the Carolina allspice bush. If you get a chance, look inside the chocolate-brown blossoms of this attractive shrub. Find out how this kind of spicebush uses beetle power to deliver pollen.

There are two main kinds of beetle flowers today. One kind has large single blossoms. Magnolias, some water lilies, dogwood, California poppies, peonies, some members of the arum family, and wild roses all attract beetles. Have you ever picked a lovely yellow pond lily and found visiting beetles inside its cup of petals? There are sometimes five or six beetles in one small lily, all feeding on nectar and sometimes nibbling pollen and stamens.

The other group of beetle flowers includes those that grow in clusters — elderberry, wild carrot (Queen Anne's lace), cow parsnip, and some kinds of sunflowers.

Most of the individual flowers that make up the clusters are rather flat, with the nectar exposed where the short-tongued beetles can lap it up. Since beetles bite and chew as well as lap, ovules in such flowers are usually protected by the fact that the ovary is buried deep inside the flower, where hungry beetles cannot reach.

Use some of your observation cages to catch and examine beetles. Look for them in and on the typical beetle flowers that are mentioned above. After you have a beetle in a bottle, add bits of flower parts, including pollen. If your beetle is hungry, you may have a chance to see how it uses its two pairs of biting jaws. Use your magnifying glass for a close look. You will see that it has no way of getting nectar out of a deep nectary. It can only lap up a drop that is exposed in a wide-open flower, just as its age-old ancestors may have lapped up sweet sap from ancient trees before there were any flowers on the earth.

Probably all modern flowers were developed from primitive ones that were pollinated by beetles. As flowers developed, insects, too, changed. Nectar-feeding insects arrived on the earth, and in time there were butterflies, moths, bees, flies, and wasps, all feeding in flowers and pollinating them. It is known from a study of fossils that flowers and nectar-feeding insects arrived on the earth at about the same time. As they lived together, as the insects fed on nectar, the flowers and insects both changed. Insects became adapted to flowers, and flowers became adapted to the insects. How this happened is not yet known, but the insects and plants that were best adapted to live in the environment survived.

Chapter

6

BEES

Bees are the insects that have adapted best to the ways of flowers. They are the most useful visitors flowers have today. Other insects come to flowers only for nectar. Each takes just the amount of nectar it needs for its own daily food. Bees, however, use both nectar and pollen for food and collect enough of both to feed their young and to store away for the winter months. A single bee from a hive will collect at least twenty-five times as much nectar as it needs for its own food, as well as great amounts of pollen. While a wasp or other nectar-feeder is visiting a few dozen flowers, a busy bee will be dipping in and out of several hundred.

The secret of a bee's continuous visiting of flowers lies in its special way of life. This is something worth investigating. Scientists have been studying bees for centuries and still do not understand how these amazing little insects are able to do all the things they do.

When we think of bees, we usually think first of the honeybees. These are the ones that have queens and live in hives, where they store food for the winter. They live in large groups, called colonies, in which each little bee

does its own job to keep the colony going. For this reason, honeybees are classed as social insects. They live
together in an organized society rather than each living
alone and having only itself to look after.

The hive in which a colony of honeybees lives serves
as a nest for eggs, a nursery for the care of the young, and
a storage place for food. It is a dry shelter for rainy days, a
home that can be kept cool in summer and warm in winter, and a safe place that can be defended from enemies.

There are three different kinds of bees in a hive. The
female bees, all except the queen, are worker bees.
There are thousands of workers in every hive. The work-
ers, as their name shows, do all the work for the colony.
They go out and gather nectar and make it into honey.
They collect pollen and mix it with honey to make bee-

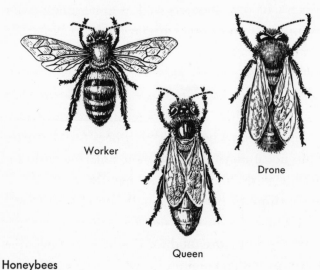

Worker

Drone

Queen

Honeybees

bread, which they feed to young bees. They make wax and mold it into cells to store food and to serve as safe places for eggs. They even collect sticky liquids from the buds of plants and make them into a kind of glue, which they use to repair weak and broken places in the cells of the hive.

Workers also take care of the young, clean the hive, guard it from enemies, use their wings as fans to keep the hive cool on hot days, and, by bunching together, create warmth in winter with heat from their little bodies. As though this were not enough, the workers also take turns looking after the personal needs of the queen, waiting on her hand and foot. A worker lives for only six weeks, and during its short life it does nothing but work, work, work.

The male bees of the hive are called drones. They have easy lives indeed, for they do no work at all. Their only value to the colony is to mate with young queens. They have short tongues, for they gather no nectar. Neither do they collect pollen. All during the warm days of spring and summer, when the workers are flying in and out of the hive with their loads of nectar and pollen, the drones stay at home, feeding on the honey the workers provide. When the nectar-gathering days are over, however, the workers are no longer willing to share food with the drones. They push the drones out of the hive. Without food or shelter, and with the cold winds beginning to blow, the drones soon die.

The third kind of bee is the queen. There is one in each hive. The queen is a large female, the largest bee in the colony. While workers live for only a few weeks and drones for only a season, a queen may live for three, four, or even five years. All her life she has only one job to do—lay eggs. She keeps busy at her job from February till late in the fall, laying as many as fifteen hundred eggs a day. Only workers hatch from the eggs that are laid early in the spring. By summer, both workers and drones come from the queen's eggs.

It takes only three days till a tiny, blind, wormlike larva comes out of an egg. The larvae are fed by the workers till they spin cocoons around themselves and become pupae. This is the sleeping-changing stage. At the end of this stage, the young bees climb out of their cocoons and begin their lives as drones or workers.

Every once in a while, however, some of the larvae are given a special kind of food. Instead of the ordinary bee-bread, they are fed on royal jelly, which is made inside the throats of young workers. For some chemical reason, the larvae that are fed on royal jelly develop not into workers and drones but into young queens.

About the time the young queens are ready to begin climbing out of their cocoons, there is a big moving day at the hive. The old queen and thousands of her loyal workers leave the hive in a great cloud. The bees swarm around empty boxes, hollow trees, and openings in the walls of buildings. They look for a new home. As soon as they find one that suits them, they settle down and go on with the life of the colony in their new hive.

Meanwhile, many workers have stayed behind to take care of the future queens that are developing in their cocoons. Most of the drones have also stayed behind. Their one hour of importance is drawing near.

When the first queen begins to emerge, the other bees stand around and watch a strange and savage ceremony. The first queen to free itself from its cocoon makes a high sound. The young queen then climbs out of her cell. If two queens emerge at the same time, they begin fighting at once. They fight until one of them is killed. The winner then goes to all of the other cells that hold future queens and stings them to death. Or if some of them are still in the larva stage, she may pull them apart with the help of some of the workers. The young queen keeps on killing until she is rid of all rival queens. The workers drag out the dead bodies and tidy up the hive.

As soon as all rival queens have been done away with, the victorious new queen leaves the hive and flies high into the air, pursued by a cloud of drones. This is the mating flight. Sooner or later, one of the drones is able to reach the high-flying queen. He becomes her mate and then dies.

The queen returns to the hive and begins her life-long activity of laying eggs. In time, her young workers will pick out some of the larvae and feed them on royal jelly. Then, while the future queens are developing, it will be her turn to leave the hive and find a new home for herself and her swarm of workers.

This whole complicated life in a hive depends entirely on flowers. Only when flowers became common on the earth could honeybees live and thrive. The worker bee is the link between flowers and the hive. To understand how bees are able to live as they do, you will want to look at the wonderful body of a worker bee.

Use one of your plastic jars to catch a flower-visiting bee. Use the suggestions for catching bees, given on page 43. Try to catch a honeybee rather than one of the huge, furry bumblebees. If it is a honeybee, you can be sure that it is one of the workers, since neither drones nor queens visit flowers. Use your magnifying glass to get a good look at the unusual parts of this amazing little animal.

Look at the thick, furry hairs that cover most of the bee's body. You can see how easily the sticky pollen grains can collect on such a fuzzy coat.

Look at the prickly, hairy legs. You may see some grains of pollen clinging to the hairs. The two front legs have special hooks that are used by the bee to clean its antennae. Notice the wide, flat places ringed with stiff hairs that are on the hind legs. These are the worker's pollen baskets. The bee collects pollen on its hairy body and in its pollen baskets, which are often packed full. When a worker gets back to the hive, it empties its baskets and scrapes the pollen from the rest of its body. Other workers receive the pollen, mix it with honey to

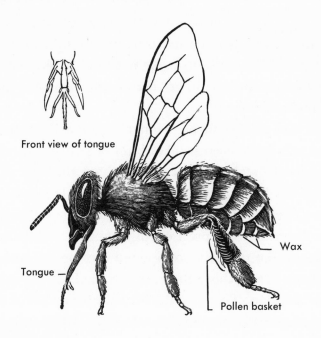

Front view of tongue

Wax

Tongue —

⌐ Pollen basket

Honeybee

make beebread, and feed it to the larvae.

Notice the four shiny wings. When a bee flies, each of the front wings hooks onto one of the rear ones. With its pair of double wings, a bee can fly forward, backward, up, down, sideways, and can hover in mid-air like a helicopter.

The mouth parts of a worker are just right for the work it does. It has a most unusual tongue. There is a little hairy spoon at the tip. This is used to spoon up nectar. The rest of the tongue forms a tube through which nectar can be sucked into the bee's body. Thus, its tongue is really a combination soup spoon and drinking straw. The bee can move its tongue up and down, back and forth, and can make it longer or shorter. No wonder bees are able to get nectar from so many different kinds of flowers!

On each side of the bee's tongue is a jaw for chewing. It uses its jaws when it takes bites of pollen and when it works the scales of wax that form on the sides of its body. The bee pulls off the scales with its legs and then chews the wax till it is soft. It then uses the soft wax to form the beautifully precise cells we find in a honeycomb.

Notice the two large compound eyes on the sides of the bee's head. Above them, in a triangle, you will see three tiny dots. These are the bee's simple eyes. You will also see its useful antennae, which it uses for smelling.

At the end of the worker's body you will see its stinger, which is its only means of defense. This is a sharp, hollow tube covered with tiny barbs like fishhooks. When a bee uses its stinger, the hooks hold the stinger in. A poison, made inside the bee's body, is forced through the stinger. When the bee flies away, the stinger is torn out of its body, and the bee dies. A queen, however, has a smooth stinger, which she can use over and over again, as she does when killing her rivals. Drones have no stingers at all.

Probably the most wonderful parts of the worker's body are inside where they cannot be seen. They are the parts that make rich, sticky honey from the watery, slightly sweet nectar the bee sips from flowers. The nectar is sucked up through the bee's tongue and into a special pouch, its "honey stomach." After the bee has

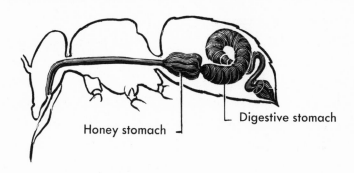

Honey stomach   Digestive stomach

Stomachs of a honeybee

visited about a hundred flowers, it has all the nectar its honey stomach can hold. With its full load, which is less than half a drop of nectar, the bee flies back to the hive. While it is flying, certain chemicals that are made in the bee's body are added to the nectar. When the bee reaches the hive, it sucks the nectar back up out of its honey stomach and puts it into a wax cell. There in the cell, water evaporates from the nectar, and the chemicals change the nectar into honey. It takes about forty thousand beeloads of nectar to make a single pound of honey.

The next time you go to a big market, look at the jars of honey. On the next page are the names of different kinds of honey found on a shelf in a California supermarket.

Clover	Mesquite
Buckwheat	Tupelo
Alfalfa	Eucalyptus
Sage	Exotic Hawaiian
Orange Blossom	Thistle
Avocado	Desert Blossom

Natural Mountain

Each jar label has a picture as well as the name of the kind of flowers from which the honey was made. Some of the jars of orange blossom honey have lovely little white orange blossoms floating inside the golden honey.

When you see honey in a market, read the labels on the jars. See how many different kinds there are. Find out where the different kinds of honey come from. You will not be surprised to find that orange blossom honey usually comes from California, where so many orange trees grow. The kinds of honey show you what flowers the workers visited while gathering nectar. The labels on the jars may also show you the part of the country in which the flowers grow.

Look also for honey in a comb. This is a square of wax cells filled with honey and held by a wood frame. If you can, buy one of the combs and spoon out some of the wax and honey. Put the spoonful into your mouth, wax and all. Taste the flowery sweetness of the honey. Chew the wax until it is soft. Then look at it and work it with your fingers. Look at the strong but delicate structure of the honeycomb and think of thousands of little worker bees using softened wax to form such perfect things as the cells of a comb.

Bees are the only insects that provide food for man. These wonderful little living factories use the raw materials in flowers and change them into a delicious product. They make honey not for us, of course, but for themselves. For this reason, people who take honey from a hive always leave plenty behind for the bees to feed them through the winter and to keep the colony going.

School children, older students, and scientists sometimes use observation hives in order to study honey-making at close range. An observation hive comes fitted with frames for honeycombs and stocked with a complete colony of live bees. Such a hive costs between forty and fifty dollars. It may be bought from one of the science supply companies listed on page 147. Such a hive has two sides of glass, covered by wood panels. The panels are taken off when the bees are being observed. The hive fits on a window sill. The worker bees fly in and out of the hive as they gather nectar and pollen from nearby flowers. Through the glass, an observer can watch the fascinating social life of the colony.

Bumblebees, like honeybees, are social insects. They, too, live in colonies but do not build hives. They live in holes in the ground, in bunches of dry grass, or even in old nests that have been deserted by field mice or other small animals. Life in a colony of bumblebees is much like life in a hive except that the queen does more than lay eggs. At first, she gathers nectar and pollen and builds a honeypot from the wax scales that form on her body. She also builds wax cells for her eggs and helps feed the larvae. After the first batch of workers has developed from larvae, however, the queen has an easier life. She settles down to being just the queen mother of the colony, laying eggs while the workers take care of her and the young.

Most other kinds of bees in the world are solitary insects. They do not live in colonies, though they often build their little nests near each other. Each female is both queen and worker. It builds the nests, lays the eggs, and collects nectar and pollen. Whether solitary or social, all bees, as you can see, depend on flowers. And the flowers they visit depend on the bees for pollination.

BEE FLOWERS

Plants whose flowers are pollinated by bees are the most successful plants on the earth today. They are sure to be pollinated, have fruits, and form seeds that will grow into good new plants each generation. As long as there are bees, such plants will survive. Think for a moment of the different things a flower must do in order to make sure that bees will take care of the job of pollination.

First, the flower must be able to attract a bee from a distance.

Second, the flower must have a way of drawing the insect right to it, of making it choose that particular flower among others that are in bloom.

Third, the flower must be able to guide the bee to a place where it cannot help touching the stamens, the stigma, or both. While inside, the bee must be well dusted with pollen.

Fourth, the flower must reward the bee for its visit and give it a good reason for visiting other flowers of the same kind.

Finally, the flowers that depend on cross-pollination must have ways of preventing self-pollination.

Bee flowers have structures that seem to be perfectly fitted to the ways of bees. How such structures developed through millions of years is a complex bit of evolution. Much investigating needs to be done to discover how it all came about.

A bee, as you know, can detect the scent of flowers. It is probably first drawn to a flower by its odor. Most bee flowers have a strong, heavy fragrance. When the bee gets near enough to see the flower, it is drawn to it by color as well as scent. You will notice that most bee flowers are yellow, blue, violet, or greenish-white.

Bees do not see all colors. Experiments with bees have shown that they see yellow, orange, and green as one color; and blue, purple, and violet as another color. They do not see red as a color. To a bee, red probably looks black or dark gray. But bees *can* see ultraviolet, a color that we cannot see at all. Greenish-white flowers and a few brilliant red flowers, like the scarlet wild poppies, probably reflect ultraviolet light. This would explain why bees do visit these red flowers, though they ignore many other red ones. In any case, bees visit the flowers of the colors they see best — the various shades of yellow, the various shades of blue, and the ultraviolets, which probably come from certain whitish or brilliant scarlet blossoms.

If you live where there are bees, you can do some investigations with color. Get some pieces of colored paper, about four inches square. Use bright blue, bright yellow, gray, black, and red. Put a table or box near a place where the bees are coming for water or for nectar. Spread the papers in a row and fasten each one down with a thumbtack. Then put a few drops of honey in the middle of the *yellow* square. Leave the other squares empty. Do this for several days so the bees will learn to come to the yellow square for honey.

Then, get a fresh, clean yellow square of the same kind of paper. Take away the one that had honey on it. Leave all the squares as before but without any honey. Move them around and watch how the bees find the yellow square. Even without the sweet-smelling honey to guide it, a bee can find its way to the yellow spot. It seems to be able to remember yellow. Bees will react the same way to certain shades of blue. Try the experiment several times, using different colors.

By putting out saucers of honey, sugar water, perfume, salt water, plain water, and marmalade, you may also find out the kinds of odors and substances that bees can detect. Watch the bees as they sip up some things and avoid others.

Bees seem to have a memory for scent and color and perhaps also for the nectar of a particular kind of flower. Once a bee gets nectar from a flower, it goes only to other flowers of the same kind as long as they are in bloom. If it feeds on clover nectar, for instance, it does not visit orange blossoms or alfalfa. A bee does not mix its nectar.

This is very fortunate for plants, for a flower can be pollinated only by its own kind of pollen. If a bee went first to clover, then to an orange blossom, and then to an alfalfa flower, much pollen would be wasted. Clover pollen will not fertilize the ovules in an orange blossom, nor will orange blossom pollen make alfalfa seeds grow. The habit of visiting only one kind of flower at a time is called flower constancy. The flower constancy of bees adds greatly to their usefulness to flowers.

The flowers, of course, are equally useful to the bees. For one thing, they provide the bees with lots of pollen. Bee flowers are great pollen producers, for, as you know, bees collect much pollen for food. If a flower had only a small amount of pollen, bees might take it all. There would be none left for the important job of pollination. But bee flowers have plenty for the bees with enough left over for themselves.

You can make a collection of bee flowers almost any day from late spring to late summer. If you live in a warm climate, you can collect throughout the fall, as long as there are any bees flying around. Use your coffee can lined with wet paper napkins for a collecting case. First, look for bees, and when you find some, watch which flowers they are visiting. Then break off one blossom of each kind and put it into your can.

After you have found a few bee flowers, bring them home and look at them carefully through your magnifying glass. Try to discover how each flower does the four or five things that most bee flowers are able to do.

Then make a record in a notebook of the things you find out. Use at least a page for each kind of flower. Write the name of the flower if you know it. Whether you know the name or not, write a description of the flower.

Smell the flower and describe its scent. Write down the color, shape, and number of petals and tell about any markings that may be nectar guides. Put down something about the way the flower grew on the plant (in clusters, with other flowers on a long stem, in spikes or flower heads, or by itself). Tell also whether it came from a small plant, a bush, vine, or tree. You may then want to make a colored picture of the whole flower as it looks from the outside.

Next, take the flower apart and make careful drawings of the inside parts. Show these things for each bee flower you find:

STAMENS: the number, shape and arrangement

POLLEN: color, amount, and ease with which it shakes off when you touch it

PISTIL: the shape and size in relation to stamens

OVARY: shape, size, and inside appearance when you cut it open

STIGMA: shape, size, and presence or absence of pollen grains on it

Look also for drops of nectar, nectaries, spurs, and the tiny hairs that sometimes grow inside.

As you study each flower, try to figure out exactly what happens when a bee catches its scent, flies toward it, and lands on its petals.

Here are the stories of some bee flowers that have special parts or unusual ways of functioning when bees come to them for nectar and pollen.

PUSSY WILLOW. Honeybees, bumblebees, and some of the wild solitary bees that are out nectar-hunting early in the spring can always get food from the pussy willow. This little tree or shrub grows wild from the East Coast to the Mississippi River. In the West, pussy willows are often found in parks and gardens. The silver-gray furry buds give the plant its name.

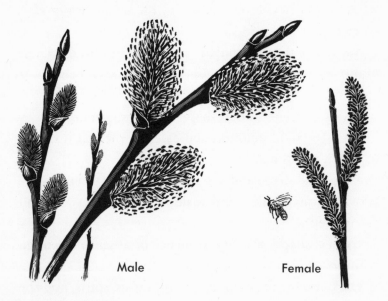

Male   Female

Pussy willow flowers

Pussy willows are among those plants having two kinds of flowers, male and female. The male flowers contain the stamens, with plenty of pollen, and a tiny bit of nectar. The female flowers also have nectar, though of course no stamens or pollen. But, since both the male and female flowers have nectar, the hungry bees fly from one to the other, pollinating as they go.

Avocado flowers

AVOCADO. Trees that bear the avocado fruit grow in warm climates. In order to bear fruit, the flowers must be cross-pollinated. Avocado pollen is too heavy and too sticky to be carried by small insects. Only large bees can do the job.

These trees have unusual structures that insure cross-pollination. One kind of avocado tree has flowers that shed pollen only in the morning. At that time, their stigmas are closed. In the afternoon, the stigmas are open, but no more pollen is released. The second kind of avocado tree has flowers that shed pollen in the afternoon and have their stigmas open in the morning. Thus, self-pollination is impossible. The pollen for the first kind of tree must come from the second kind, and vice versa. This means that avocado growers must be sure that the bees can reach both kinds of tree. Otherwise, the flowers will not be pollinated, no seeds will develop, and there will be no fruits.

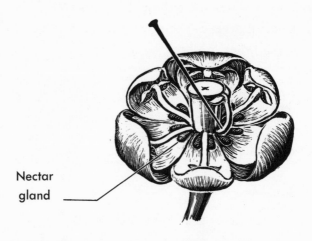

Nectar
gland

Stamen in barberry flower moving when pressed by a pin

BARBERRY. There are several kinds of barberries. They are low shrubs with sharp spines on the stems. They grow wild in the East, and in many places in the country are planted to form hedges along walks and in gardens. In the spring they have clusters of small yellow flowers.

If you look closely at one of the little barberry blossoms, you will see that each of the six stamens opens in a T-shape to shed the pollen. You will also see two tiny orange nectar glands at the base of each stamen. Nectar comes out of the glands and collects around the bottom of the stamens. When a bee pushes its tongue into the nectar, it touches the base of a stamen. The stamen immediately curves over the bee and dusts its back with pollen. As soon as the bee leaves the flower, the stamen returns to its original position, ready for the next bee.

If you have a barberry flower, you can see how its moving stamens work by using a pin as the bee uses its tongue. Just press the point of the pin against the bottom of one of the stamens. The stamen will move toward the center of the flower. When you take away the pin, the stamen will move back. You may want to try this experiment with some other kinds of flowers. Some cactus flowers also move their inside parts when they are touched by the tongue of a bee.

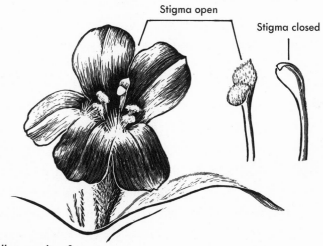

Stigma open

Stigma closed

Yellow monkey flower

YELLOW MONKEY FLOWER. These are also called sticky monkey flowers or mimulus. They grow wild on the

Western plains and mountains, covering the land in spring with patches of egg-yolk yellow. Some mimulus, in a variety of colors, are also raised in other areas as garden flowers.

Look inside one of the sticky monkey flowers. Use your magnifying glass. You will see four deep yellow stamens, two of them short and two of them long. On the tip of each is a two-lobed pollen sac that looks like a tiny golden heart. Above the stamens and close to the inside of the upper petal, you will find a most unusual stigma. It is diamond-shaped and silvery-white. It seems to be slim, flat, and dry — not at all like the moist, cushiony stigmas found in most flowers.

When the stigma is ready to receive pollen, however, the little diamond splits open from top to base. The inside is moist and lined with long, silky hairs. You can see how the stigma operates by holding your hands flat together, middle fingers pointing upward. Then, with your wrists tight together, open your hands outward. This is the way the monkey flower stigma opens to receive pollen.

When a bee enters the flower, it has to brush against the open stigma. Some grains of pollen are scraped off onto it. The stigma closes at once. Sometimes it closes so fast that it seems almost to snap shut. At other times, the two parts of the stigma fold slowly over the pollen grains like two hands clasping something in a double fist.

Meanwhile, the bee is busy feeding on nectar and getting more pollen on its legs and back. When it moves out of the flower, it cannot leave pollen on the stigma because it is still closed. In this way, the monkey flower protects itself from self-pollination.

Find a monkey flower with an open stigma. Touch the stigma with a pin. The two "hands" will fold shut. But wait! In a few minutes, they will open again. They do not stay closed because you gave them no pollen. Now, take a pinch of pollen from another kind of flower — a rose, lupine, lily, or any other kind. With your pin, put some pollen onto the open stigma. Again, the stigma will close. And again, it will open after a few moments. What is wrong this time? It received pollen but not the right kind. Next, try pollen from another monkey flower. This should make the stigma stay closed, just as it does after it has received a good dose of monkey flower pollen from a bee.

If you live where catalpa trees grow (you may call them "lady cigars" because of their long seed pods), look at their flowers. Try some investigations with a pin and with different kinds of pollen. You will find that catalpa flowers act very much like the flowers of the monkey flower plant.

SCOTCH BROOM. Several kinds of bright yellow broom grow wild and in gardens all over the United States. Their flowers can be pollinated only by a heavy insect. Bumblebees usually do the job.

The bottom lip of the flower serves as a kind of landing platform. When a bumblebee comes in for a landing, its weight pushes the lip down. The flower then springs open, and five short stamens spring out and dust the bee's belly. Then some long stamens spring out and dust the bee's back. The stamens seem to be just the right length to curve all around a big bumblebee.

Find some broom plants in bloom. With your finger or with a pencil, push down on the bottom lip of a flower. Look at the little cloud of pollen that comes from the stamens! Broom flowers have plenty of pollen for the bees but no nectar at all. The bee is probably attracted to the flower by the bright yellow color. Once it lands, it follows a red nectar guide that leads it to . . . no nectar! Instead of finding a sweet drink, the bee is caught by the stamens and given a good dusting. It seems almost as though the flower is playing a trick on the bumblebee.

Before

After

Alfalfa flowers

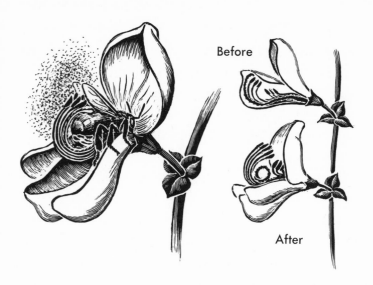

Before

After

Bumblebee in broom blossom

However, bees can always use pollen, and broom flowers certainly give them plenty of it.

ALFALFA. This is one of our most important hay crops. Without alfalfa, many cattle would be thin and hungry. Like most bee flowers, alfalfa blossoms offer both nectar and pollen.

In the little alfalfa blossom, the pistil and stamens, as well as the nectar, are tucked up inside. When a bee lands on the flower, POP! Out come the pistil and stamens, covering the bee with pollen from the tips of its feelers to the end of its stinger. Only after the flower has popped open can the bee go on in for a sip of nectar. However, the flower does not depend on cross-pollination. The movement of the nectar-seeking bee shakes the blossom's own pollen onto its waiting stigma.

It is known that honeybees are able to steal nectar from alfalfa blossoms without making them pop. For this reason, they are not very good alfalfa pollinators. There are certain kinds of wild bees, however, that do not seem to mind getting a pollen bath. Farmers depend mainly on wild bees to make the alfalfa flowers pop open. Then the flowers pollinate themselves.

Red clover and bumblebee

RED CLOVER. Red clover depends entirely on bumble-bees for its pollination. Wherever you see the fuzzy, fragrant blossoms of red clover, you will find their partners, the bumblebees. The clover-bumblebee partnership is important for cattle and for all of us who like milk, butter, cheese, and beef.

Long ago there was no red clover growing in New Zealand, which is a large island in the Pacific. Much live-stock was being raised there, and the ranchers were in-terested in improving their hay crops. They imported red clover seed from Europe. The clover was planted, and it grew well. The plants became strong and tall, and the purplish blossoms filled the air with fragrance. The ranchers were proud of their first crop of red clover and looked forward to other good crops in future years. In Europe, as in the United States, red clover, once it gets a good start, keeps reseeding itself year after year.

In New Zealand, however, the second year's crop was thin and poor. The red clover, in spite of its good start, was dying out. The ranchers were disappointed and puz-zled. Why, they wondered, could they not raise good red clover in New Zealand?

You may have guessed what the trouble was. There were no bumblebees in New Zealand. None at all. And so the red clover was not being properly pollinated. Once the mystery had been solved, one hundred British bumblebees were brought to New Zealand and put into the clover fields. The bees went right to work, and to-day there are plenty of red clover plants and plenty of bumblebees in New Zealand.

The next time you see a red clover blossom, look at it closely. Pull it apart with your fingers. You will find that what we call the clover flower is really a whole bunch of flowers growing on a single stem. Each of the tiny flow-ers, or florets, has seed-making parts, with a bit of nectar inside. When a bumblebee lights on a clover head, it moves rapidly over its surface, bobbing its head up and down as it dips into one floret after another. After it has pushed its tongue into all the florets on one flower head, it flies on to the next. If you have patience and good eyesight, you can count the number of florets one bumblebee dips into in a ten-minute period. A single bumblebee has been reported to go into as many as eight hundred florets in a single hour!

Vanilla orchid

VANILLA. This is a plant you will not be able to find because it grows only in Mexico and in other tropical lands. But, if you like the flavor of vanilla in ice cream and other sweets, you may be interested in finding out about the flowers and fruits of the vanilla plant.

When Cortez, the Spanish conqueror, entered Mexico more than four hundred years ago, he found the Aztec people using vanilla to flavor their food. He learned that the flavor came from the fruit or bean pod — of an orchid plant. Later, other adventurers saw the orchids on which vanilla pods grew and brought cuttings of the plants back to Europe. The cuttings were planted in rich soil and kept in warm, moist greenhouses. They grew well and in time bore flower buds.

The buds opened, covering the vines with orchid blossoms — delicate yellow-green flowers. The flowers opened early in the morning, but by the middle of the afternoon of the same day they withered, faded, and fell off the vines. There was not a single seed pod, though the plants continued to grow well. There were lovely flowers twice each year but never any fruits. For three hundred years after Cortez first discovered vanilla, it was impossible to grow the bean pods anywhere except in the plant's native land.

Do you know what was lacking? You have probably guessed that the flowers could not pollinate themselves. They needed help from some insect that lived only where the vanilla orchid grew naturally. The insect was a tiny stingless bee that is common in Mexico but not in other places. The secret was discovered more than a hundred years ago by a French plant scientist. He took pollen from the inside of a vanilla orchid flower and pressed it onto the stigma of the same flower. He did the job the bees had been doing in Mexico. Beans grew from the flowers he pollinated.

When man takes a hand in transferring pollen, the process is called artificial pollination. This is the process now used in raising vanilla beans even on the vanilla plantations in Mexico. The little stingless bee, however, is the natural partner of the vanilla-bean orchid.

Artificial pollination is used in growing many kinds of plants, especially in greenhouses and nurseries. But in the great fruit orchards of the Northwest, where there are millions of little blossoms to be pollinated every spring, man could hardly do the job. Even the local bees cannot get around to all the flowers on the trees in large orchards. And so, special crews of workers are brought in — worker bees from hives that the orchard owners rent for the occasion. Beekeeping is a business. There are many thousands of beekeepers in the United States. They sell honey and also each spring rent out hives to the orchard owners. In this way, the worker bees get all the nectar and pollen they need for their hives, and the orchard owners get the extra help they need for the pollination of their fruit trees. It is indeed a good partnership.

8

BUTTERFLIES AND MOTHS AND THE FLOWERS THEY VISIT

The best place to watch for butterflies is beside a buddleia plant. Buddleia has flowers so attractive to butterflies that it is commonly called a butterfly bush. Butterfly bushes are grown in gardens all over the United States. They are rather low shrubs in the colder climates, but where the weather is warm all year long, they often grow to be fifteen feet tall.

And what flowers! In late summer and through the fall, they bear long spikes of purplish blooms. Each spike, made up of hundreds of small trumpet-shaped flowers, sends out waves of fragrance. All the butterflies in the neighborhood get the message and gather around the sweet-smelling bush. They flit, hover, and dart, as they sip nectar from the long, thin flower tubes.

Watch a butterfly drift gracefully to a blossom and perch daintily on its edge. Watch it cling to the petals with its slender legs. Watch it uncoil its long tongue and dip it into a flower.

If you move very quickly, you may be able to sweep a butterfly into one of your largest plastic jars. Sweep the insect off its feet while it is perched on a flower or sweep

Buddleia, or butterfly bush, with butterflies

it out of the air while it is flying. Then put a bright, sweet-smelling flower into the jar with the butterfly and watch the insect climb onto the flower and cling to its petals.

Notice the insect's large compound eyes. Some butterflies have as many as twenty thousand separate lenses in each eye. Butterflies have good vision (for insects) and are greatly attracted to colors. Unlike bees, butterflies can see red as a color. They can also see other bright colors.

Look at the butterfly's antennae. They are usually very slender, with dots or knobs on the tips. A butterfly uses its antennae for both smelling and hearing. It has a keen sense of smell, which guides it to fragrant flowers.

Look at the wings. As you know, they get their lovely colors and patterns from thousands of tiny scales that are arranged in overlapping rows, like shingles on a roof. The wings are large for the insect's body and fine for flying.

Look at the long, wobbly legs. Most butterflies *can* walk, after a fashion, if they need to, but they prefer to fly. The slender legs are used mainly for clinging as the insect hangs onto a flower.

You have heard many times that adult insects have six legs. Now, as you look at your specimen, you *may* see only four legs. If you look more closely, however, you will find a pair of tiny front ones curled up close to the butterfly's body. Some kinds of butterflies have very short front legs, which they use mainly for wiping their faces and combing their hair.

Use your magnifying glass to get a good look at the butterfly's mouth parts. You will find no biting or chewing jaws but only a long tongue, which the insect carries coiled up in a neat little spring under its chin. The tongue is a hollow tube through which the insect gets all its food. A butterfly has no choice but to live on a liquid diet all of its butterfly days. Its liquid food is the nectar in flowers.

Butterflies have a keen chemical sense. They can tell sugar water from plain water even when there is only a tiny, tiny amount of sugar in the water. We are not able

Monarch butterfly, adult and chrysalis

to do this, but they can do it easily. This is important for them, for their food comes from the tiny amounts of sweetness in nectar. Butterflies would have trouble, indeed, if they could not tell a drop of nectar from a drop of rain or dew.

When you have finished looking at the butterfly, take the jar and open it near a flowering plant. The insect will find its way out of the jar and onto one of the flowers, where perhaps you will see it uncoil its tongue and begin to feed.

Butterflies feed from many of the bright-colored flowers that bloom by day. There are very few gay flowers in gardens or fields that are not visited by them. Many typical butterfly flowers are red, deep pink, or orange, since butterflies see these colors very well. Most butterfly flowers smell sweet, for butterflies are drawn by fragrance as well as by color. Wild pinks, which grow in fields and meadows, are among the favorites. They hold their nectar at the bottom of a long tube, where only a long-tongued insect can reach it.

Purple loosestrife, a butterfly flower that grows wild in many damp places and which is also planted in gardens, is worth looking for. It has dozens of small blossoms on each of its handsome, showy spikes. The small blos-

Butterfly wing scales and butterfly head

One   Two   Three

Stamens and pistils in three types of loosestrife flowers

soms have five petals and a long, thin nectar tube. The unusual thing about this plant is that it has three different types of flowers, with pistils and stamens in three assorted sizes.

Type one has *long* and *short* stamens, with a pistil of *medium* length.

Type two has *short* and *medium*-length stamens, with a *long* pistil.

Type three has *medium*-length and *long* stamens, with a *short* pistil.

A loosestrife flower with a long pistil can be pollinated only with pollen from a long stamen. One with a medium-length pistil needs pollen from a medium-length stamen. And a short pistil must be pollinated from a short stamen. You can easily see that the flowers of each type can be pollinated only with pollen from one of the other two types. They have to be cross-pollinated, and butterflies do the job.

If someone asked you whether there are more butterflies or more moths in the world, what would you say? Many people would guess that the butterflies outnumber the moths. This is because we *see* more butterflies. There are, however, far more kinds of moths than butterflies. But since most moths fly by night, we are less aware of them than we are of butterflies, which are active in the bright sunshiny hours. When darkness comes, butterflies hide and rest. Most moths, on the other hand, rest in the daytime. They stir themselves in the early hours of dusk, right after the sun has set. They do their feeding by night. At dawn, when the sky grows pale, most moths disappear.

The easiest way to catch a moth is to stand near an outdoor electric light some warm evening. Moths are attracted to the light and will fly against it even when the light is hot enough to burn their wings. Another way to attract the night-flying moths is to paint a tree trunk with syrup, for moths are also drawn to something sweet. You should be able to scoop a moth right into one of your observation cages.

When you examine moths, you will see that some have bodies that are heavier and more furry than the body of a butterfly. A few moths have bright-colored wings, but most have wings that are less brilliant than butterfly wings. Look at the moth's antennae. They are often feathery and do not have knobs at the tips. Like butterflies, moths use their antennae for smelling and hearing. Their sense of smell is even keener than that of butterflies.

Look at the tongue of the moth. Some have tongues
that are as long as their bodies. They carry them coiled
up as butterflies do.

Since most moths fly by night, they are not attracted
to bright colors. The next time you are out at night,

Hawk moth

Moth head and moth wing scales

look at some flowers. Look at red flowers, yellow ones, blue ones, white ones. What colors can you see?

Even on a bright moonlit night, you will not be able to see which colors are which. Bright red, blue, and green will look dark in the moonlight. Pale yellow and white will look silvery. You will not be able to tell the

Evening primrose

pale yellow from the white. You will not be able to tell
the red from the blue. But you will be able to tell the
pale colors from the bright, deep ones. You will discover
that you can see the pale colors best. We think this is the
way it is with moths, too. They visit most the flowers that
are pure white, creamy white, and pale yellow. Such
flowers are easiest to find at night, when the only light

Morning glory flower

is the small amount that comes from the moon and from far-off stars.

Moths, however, do not depend entirely on vision to find their way. Most of them are guided to the night-blooming flowers by their sense of smell. Flowers that bloom at night usually have a strong, heavy fragrance. In the moist night air, flower smells are carried great distances. A moth has little trouble following a scent to a night-blooming flower.

There are many flowers that depend on moths for pollination. They are flowers that bloom at night or in the early morning and the evening hours. Most of them, though not all, are pale in color and have a strong fragrance. Many have nectar at the bottom of a long flower tube. Here are some of the most common moth flowers. Find out which ones grow where you live.

yellow columbine	datura
tobacco	morning-glory
yucca	white catchfly
honeysuckle	bladder campion
phlox	night-blooming cereus
fragrant stock	bindweed
evening primrose (some kinds)	trumpet vine
night-blooming cactus	jimsonweed

When a beetle comes to a flower for a sip of nectar, it walks into an open flower, stands on the petals, and lowers its mouth into an open nectary to drink. When a bee goes to a flower, it crawls in, often pushing apart the petals of a closed flower in order to enter. It forces its hairy, furry body among the stamens as it settles down for a sip of nectar, which it can reach with its long tongue.

When a butterfly sips nectar, it usually rests on the petals or on some other part of the flower as it sips. A hawk moth, however, merely hovers over the flower as it takes in nectar through its long, hollow tongue. It does not sit down to its meals. Sometimes it is only the moth's tongue that collects grains of pollen and transfers them from one flower to the next. However, many moth flowers have very long stamens and pistils, which stick out beyond the petals. As a moth flies among such flowers, getting ready to dip its drinking-straw tongue into a flower tube, the stamens and pistils brush against its furry body.

Both butterflies and moths, like bees, have the habit of flower constancy. They visit only one kind of flower at a time. As long as that kind is in bloom, they do not change their diet. In this way, pollen is carried from one flower to another of the same kind. The pollen is carried to a place where it can do some good for the plants. Next to bees, butterflies and moths are the best cross-pollinators in the world. They help to keep the world filled with millions of bright, sweet-smelling flowers and millions of useful plants. It is a true partnership, because the flowers keep the moths and butterflies filled with nectar.

At an earlier stage in their life cycle, butterflies and

moths are not good plant partners. In fact, many of them are plant enemies. Have you ever seen a cabbage patch in which the caterpillars of the pale cabbage butterflies have been feeding? The crisp outer leaves and the tender white hearts of the cabbages are ragged, tattered, and riddled with holes. This is because the dainty little cabbage butterfly lays its eggs on cabbage plants. When the hungry caterpillars hatch from the eggs, they are surrounded by all the food they need — cabbage leaves.

This is the way with most of the Lepidoptera. They lay their eggs on a plant that will provide food for the caterpillars when they hatch out. Monarch butterflies, a common kind in North America, choose milkweed plants. Some butterflies and moths lay eggs where their larvae can feed on fruits like tomatoes and apples. Most of them lay eggs on leaves or stems.

When the caterpillars hatch, they use their jaws to bite, tear, and chew their food. They eat continuously and grow fast. When a caterpillar reaches its full size, it suddenly stops eating. It makes itself a kind of cradle for its next stage of development.

Moth caterpillars spin silken cocoons around their bodies. A butterfly caterpillar makes a chrysalis. It simply curls itself up and hangs itself from a leaf or twig with a thread of silk. With some species, little golden dots appear on the body, which now becomes a chrysalis. The word, chrysalis, comes from the Greek word for gold.

Inside its cocoon or chrysalis, the insect becomes a

pupa, sealed away from the world. It neither moves nor eats. It seems dead. But it is far from dead. Wonderful things are happening to it. It is losing its fat caterpillar body. It is growing two pairs of splendid wings and three pairs of slender jointed legs. When the change is complete, the insect works its way out of its chrysalis or cocoon. It is now a fully developed butterfly or moth.

At first it does not try to fly. Its wings are damp and crumpled. It hangs or perches on a twig or blade of grass and slowly moves its wings back and forth, drying them in the air. When its wings are dry, the insect takes off, fluttering, soaring, dipping, looping — and searching for its first meal.

You can find out more about butterflies and moths by catching a caterpillar. Look for them on the plants on which they feed. Here are some of the butterflies and moths that are common all over the United States. Listed with each are some places to look for their caterpillars.

COMMON BUTTERFLIES

Name of butterfly	*Where to look for caterpillars*
Monarch	On milkweed plants
Fritillary	On goldenrods, violets, and other wild flowers
Mourning Cloak	On leaves of elm, poplar, and willow trees
Painted Lady	On burdock, thistles, nettles, and sunflowers

Cabbage	On cabbages and on the leaves of wild mustard plants
Sulphur	On clover, alfalfa, and other plants of the pea family
Swallowtail	On leaves of orange and other citrus trees, on spicebushes, parsley, wild cherry, and pipe vines

COMMON MOTHS

Name of moth	*Where to look for caterpillars*
Sphinx (or Hawk)	On potato plants, grape vines, and on the leaves of willow, birch, and catalpa trees
Polyphemus	On oak, hickory, elm, maple, and birch trees
Isabella (or Banded Woolly Bear)	On plantain and similar weeds
Codling	Inside apples and on the bark of apple trees
Corn-Ear Worm (or Bollworm)	In ears of corn
Fall Webworm	In webs that the caterpillars spin around the leaves of trees in the fall
Tent Caterpillar	In webs that the caterpillars spin between the limbs of trees in the spring

When you catch a caterpillar, put it into a large glass jar with plenty to eat and some twigs to climb on. Feed it from the kind of plant it was on when you found it. Put in fresh food each day and keep the jar clean. Watch the caterpillar often. You may be able to see it spin its cocoon or hang itself up and become a chrysalis.

Keep the cocoon or chrysalis till the pupa stage is over and the adult insect comes out. Some remain pupae for weeks, some for months. Sooner or later, a moth will work its way out of a cocoon or a butterfly will crawl out when its chrysalis splits open. After you have seen the wonderful process of change from caterpillar to pupa and from pupa to the adult winged insect, turn the butterfly or moth free and watch it as it finds its way to a sweet-smelling flower.

If you cannot find any caterpillars where you live, you may want to order a chrysalis or cocoon from one of the companies that sell live specimens to students and scientists. You will find the names and addresses of several companies on page 147. However, it is more fun (and much less expensive!) to find your own live caterpillars and take care of them till they change into butterflies or moths.

Chapter

9

THE YUCCA AND ITS PARTNER

What a strange-looking pair—the tall plant with its spike of waxy white blossoms and the tiny moth with its glistening white wings! The plant is a yucca, a member of the lily family. The moth is a Pronuba, often called, simply, a yucca moth. As different as they are in every way, the yucca plant and the Pronuba moth have a highly successful partnership. Each one is completely dependent on the other for reproduction.

The yucca cannot grow seeds without the aid of the Pronuba. No other insect, not even another kind of moth, can do what the Pronuba does for the yucca. Not only that, but each kind of yucca has its own special kind of Pronuba moth.

The Pronuba, too, is completely dependent. It cannot reproduce without its particular kind of yucca plant. It depends on the yucca for hatching its eggs and raising its young. The plant is a kind of incubator, nurse, and baby-sitter for the young moths.

Without these special services from the yucca, Pronuba moths would soon die out. Without special services from the moth, yucca plants would soon die out. This complete partnership between a plant and a moth is a beautifully developed arrangement.

Yucca plants grow wild on the dry hillsides and in the deserts of the Southwest. Spanish settlers called them "Candles of God" when they saw the white spikes of flowers rising straight and tall from bases of stiff, spread-out leaves.

During the winter season, you see only the dark, gray-green leaves, which fan out from the center like swords that have been stuck, hilt-first, into the soil. From these needle-sharp leaves has come another name for the yucca: Spanish bayonet. In winter, a tall, dead stalk, left over from last year's flowering, rises from the middle of the swordlike leaves.

Yucca plants in bloom

Early in the spring, the plant grows a new flower stalk. Up, up, up it grows till it is six, eight, or ten feet tall. On the stalk hang creamy-white blossoms, like bells that are pinched shut at the bottoms. Each of the bells is about two inches across and perhaps three inches long. There may be a hundred bells or even more growing out from a single flower stalk. From a distance, the towering white spears do indeed look like giant candles, rising from low candleholders that have been scattered across the spring-green hills.

At dusk and in the darkness of night, the yuccas seem to glow. Their waxen whiteness reflects the last faint light of day and the pale lights from moon and stars. In the deserts and on the mountainsides, yucca flowers at night stand out whitely against the dark. In this way, the yucca is like many other moth flowers — pale flowers blooming in the night for pale moths that fly after sundown.

During most of its flowering time, the yucca keeps its blossoms shut. Few insects can make their way through the pinched-up petals to the flower chamber. Any that do will receive nothing for their efforts, for the yucca has no nectar. Nor does the casual visitor serve the plant. Yucca can be pollinated only by the Pronuba.

Inside the creamy-white bells, the seed-making parts get ready for the work they will have to do. The pistil grows long and ripe for the pollen. The ovary grows fat with ovules ready to be fertilized. The stamens grow out, with soft yellow pollen ripening on the tips.

While the flower is making ready for its special work, the moth is also making ready. It has awakened inside its cocoon and has worked its way out. It has dried its dainty wings and has tried them, fluttering about in search of a mate. It has mated and is now ready to lay eggs. It is only the female moth that will visit the yucca. The males die soon after the mating.

Sometimes the egg-heavy Pronuba waits for several days, sometimes for a week or even two. Then, one evening, the pinched-up petals of the yucca blossoms unfold. Slowly, each bell opens, moving its six petals farther and farther apart. The petals bend outward and then curve upward, exposing the stamens and the pistil for the first and last time.

As the blossoms open, a strong, heavy fragrance spreads into the night air. The little Pronuba catches the scent and alerts itself for a series of complicated and unusual tasks. First, it flies to a yucca blossom. It is probably guided there by the glimmer of white and by the inviting fragrance. Certainly it is the fragrance that has given the signal to the moth that all is ready. But ready for what? Most insects go to flowers for nectar, which they can taste and for which they may feel something like hunger. The Pronuba, however, does not feed. It is not led to the flower by its need for food. It has no mouth parts for chewing and no tongue for sipping. Instead, it has a very special kind of mouth — not for feeding but for scraping up pollen. Under its chin grow two little curved parts that look like an extra pair of feelers. They are called palpi.

When the Pronuba reaches the blossom, it goes at once to the tip of a stamen and begins, with its palpi, to scrape up grains of pollen, which it pushes and kneads as a baker kneads dough for bread. Finally, the pollen is worked into a smooth, neatly shaped ball nearly three times as big as the moth's head. It tucks the ball under its chin and holds it there with its palpi.

With its pollen ball safely held, the moth leaves its blossom and flutters to another open flower. It crawls into the second flower and presses the end of its egg-laying tube against the fat ovary. It makes a little hole in the ovary wall and lays four or five eggs among the ovules. All during the egg-laying process, the little moth holds tightly to the ball of pollen.

When the eggs have been laid, the moth has one final act. This act provides for future Pronubas and for future yucca plants. The moth climbs to the stigma on the end of the pistil. This means that it climbs *down* or *out* to the pistil's end, for the blossoms hang downward from the stalk. When the moth reaches the end of the pistil, it crams the pollen ball into the stigma and then flies off into the night. It has completed its life work.

Within the ovary of the yucca, the ovules are fertilized by material from the pollen. They begin to grow into seeds. At the same time, the caterpillars inside the

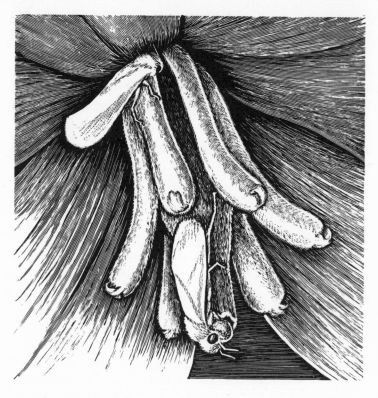

Pronuba, above, getting ready to lay eggs. Pronuba, below, putting pollen ball into stigma.

tiny moth eggs are also growing. In about four days they crawl out of their eggs and begin to feed on the young seeds.

The petals of the flower dry and fall off the seed pod. The seed pod continues to grow. It becomes large and hard as the seeds ripen inside. If you cut open a green yucca pod crosswise, you will see the flat seeds stacked neatly in three pockets, two stacks to a pocket. Inside the pockets you will also see the four or five little caterpillars in the holes they have eaten in the stacks of seeds. Each caterpillar eats about twenty seeds. Since the seed pod has an average of about two hundred seeds, there are enough left over to grow into new yucca plants.

By the time the seeds are ripe, or even before, the caterpillars are fully grown. Then each one bites a hole in the seed pod and escapes. It crawls into the fresh air for the first time in its life.

As it comes out, the caterpillar spins a thread of silk, on which it lowers itself gently to the ground. It then digs a hole in the soil and crawls in. It curls up inside the hole and spins a cocoon around itself. It stays in its cocoon for the rest of the spring and all of the summer and winter. Its pupa stage is a long one.

By the following spring, the pupa stage is ended. The Pronubas have changed into adult moths. They crawl

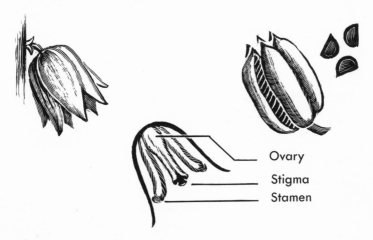

Ovary
Stigma
Stamen

Yucca flower, seed pod, and seeds

out of their cocoons and find mates. The females are then ready for the one night when the yucca blossoms open, which usually comes no more than two weeks after the moths have emerged from their cocoons. And so, the strange partnership continues.

There are many mysteries about the yucca-Pronuba partnership. Why does the yucca perfume attract only this one kind of moth? What keeps other night-flying insects from interfering with the delicate work of the little Pronuba?

What leads the Pronuba to gather pollen and roll it into a ball? Other moths are not pollen-gatherers, nor do others have a set of palpi for scraping together and holding the pollen.

What makes the moth go to a second flower to lay its eggs and so serve the yucca by cross-pollinating it?

What controls the number of eggs that are laid and the number of seeds in the seed pod? The numbers seem to be nicely balanced for a fifty-fifty partnership. On an average, one hundred seeds are used by the caterpillars and one hundred left for the plant. What accounts for this even balance?

Above all, how can we explain the miracle of timing? On the one and only night when the yucca opens its flowers, its own kind of Pronuba moth is waiting, ready to lay its eggs. If the flowers opened while the moth was still in its cocoon, the ovules would not be fertilized and seeds would not develop. If the moth were ready to lay eggs before the yucca flowers opened, the life cycles of both moth and plant would be incomplete. But these dire things do not happen. They do not happen because of a pattern of activity that we can watch but cannot understand. The moth is ready when the flowers open, and the life cycles continue over and over, year after year after year.

10

FLIES AND FLY-TRAPPING PLANTS

There are several kinds of flies that are typical flower partners. They sip nectar and fly from flower to flower much as bees do. They often look so much like bees that one must count the wings to make sure they are really flies. Flies, as you know, have only one pair of wings. When you think of flies, you think first of the common housefly with its shiny black or gray body. Houseflies, however, are insect pests, while the nectar-feeding flies are beneficial, or useful, insects.

Look for drone flies around the flowers of wild carrot (Queen Anne's lace) and English ivy. The insects have small bodies marked with yellow and black and a single pair of triangle-shaped wings. Their tongues are longer than those of most flies but not long enough to reach nectar at the bottom of deep flower tubes. They visit mainly the flat, wide-open blossoms. On the small flowers that bloom on English ivy vines, flies can lick off the sweet drops that collect on the surface.

You can catch and handle a drone fly, for, of course, it has no stinger. However, before you touch one of these

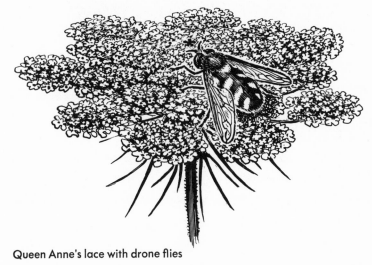

Queen Anne's lace with drone flies

hovering insects, be sure that it *is* a fly and not a worker bee.

Look also for the cousin of the drone fly, the hover or bee fly, which has a round, fuzzy body covered with black and gold hairs. It looks much like a bumblebee. Most bee flies have tongues that are at least a half inch long. They can go fairly deep for nectar. Bee flies gather around many kinds of sweet-smelling blue, violet, and yellow flowers.

The interesting thing about the nectar-feeding flies is that they seem to be imitating bees. Their tongues are

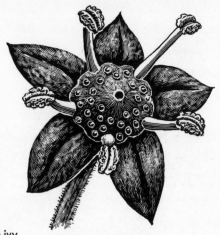

Flower of English ivy

longer than those of other flies; they have hairs on their bodies, on which pollen collects; they use nectar for food; and their feeding habits serve flowers by pollinating them. Their wings, however, give them away. They are typical of insects of the order Diptera, to which they belong.

One of the favorite plants of nectar-feeding flies is the speedwell, or Veronica. Veronicas are sometimes found growing in lawns as weeds. Their leaves are gray-green and often fuzzy. The tiny flowers, a deep lavender-blue, grow on spikes that bend over at the tips. Other kinds of Veronicas are tall plants that are grown as garden flowers. When an individual flower opens, two stamens stick out. A visiting fly holds onto the stamens when it lands on the flower and thus takes on a load of pollen. When it goes to the next Veronica blossom, it leaves pollen on its stigma.

If you can find a Veronica plant, use your magnifying glass to look inside the tiny flowers that make up the spike. Find the nectar guides, dark lines leading to a white spot in the center, where the nectar is found.

Except for the bee-imitators, flies have an unusual relationship with flowers. Small mosquitoes, gnats, midges, and other tiny flies are lured to a flower by some kind of bait, then trapped and held prisoner until the job of pollination has been done. A good example of a fly-trapping flower is the lady's-slipper, or moccasin flower, an

Stamens
Stigma

Lady's-slipper

orchid that grows wild in many parts of the United States. The lovely white and pink lady's-slipper is the state flower of Minnesota. There are also large, brilliant yellow lady's-slippers and small white ones. Lady's-slippers are found in moist meadows and woodlands.

This kind of orchid gets its name from its lowest petal, which is a hollow sac shaped like a slipper or moccasin. On each side of the sac are two winglike petals and, above it, a single graceful petal with clearly marked nectar guides. The inside of the slipper part is smooth and slick, except at the end, or heel. There you will find a patch of rough hairs, like a tiny door mat. A small fly enters the slipper and becomes trapped in the toe. It cannot climb up the steep, slick inside walls, and the opening is too small for the insect to fly through. Its feet finally clutch the hairs on the tiny mat, where it is able to get a grip. It then works its way along the heel. This carpeted hallway leads the fly to the seed-making parts, where it hits the stigma first and then the stamens. When the fly touches the stamens, they release a whole mass of pollen grains that are especially sticky. They cling to the fly's body as it makes its way out through a kind of back door, flies away from the flower, and then down into the next lady's-slipper it can find. In the second flower, it leaves pollen from the first as it hits the stigma at the start of its climb through the flower's heel.

Many flies, as you know, feed on dead and decaying animal material. Some flowers have foul smells that at-

tract such flies. The arum lily, for instance, smells like
carrion and appeals to carrion-feeding flies. Sticking up
in the middle of each arum flower is a tall, fleshy part
that actually heats up when the flower is ready to be pollinated. The heat helps to spread the odor, inviting flies
in the neighborhood to drop in for a meal of rotting
meat. This, of course, is one of the arum's tricky ways,
for there is no meat at all for the flies.

However, the flies answer the flower's invitation and
drop in (literally!) by the score. Gnats and other tiny
flies are common guests. Once they touch the sides of
the flower's deep cup, down they go to the bottom on a
slide made slippery with tiny droplets of oil. The flies
slide through a ring of stiff, brushlike hairs that keep
larger insects out. They cannot climb back up the slippery wall, nor can they climb up the center part of the
flower because of the stiff hairs.

Inside the arum, there is a ring of female flowers
around the bottom, with a ring of male flowers growing
above them. The trapped insects crawl around on the
female flowers, where they find drops of sweet liquid.
While they are lapping up the sweet stuff, the stamens
on the male flowers above them open up and rain down
a shower of pollen.

The brushlike hairs that have been prison bars to the
insects begin to soften after pollen has been shed. As the
hairs wilt, the gnats and other small creatures can crawl
up the middle part of the flower and then fly away. Away

they go, not to freedom in the open air, but to another
arum flower, to which they are lured once more by the
tempting smell of rotting meat. Again they are captured,
and this time they leave pollen from the first flower on
the stigmas inside their new prison. This goes on as long
as there are arums in bloom.

Dutchman's-pipe and other pipe-vine flowers attract
flies much as arum lilies do. When a Dutchman's-pipe
is in bloom, it sends out an unpleasant odor — unpleasant to us but very inviting to gnats and other small flies.
When a fly touches the inside of the blossom, which is
shaped like the bowl of an old-fashioned pipe, it slides
down to the bottom. This time, it is wax rather than oil
that makes the slide slippery. Inside the lower part of
the flower there are many hairs, all pointing downward.
The tiny insects cannot crawl back up through the hairs,
and so they stay trapped in the deep part of the flower
tube. They are kept there for several days and probably
do not try to escape since there is plenty of nectar for
them to feed on. Finally, the stamens release pollen and
give the flies a thorough dusting. Then the down-pointing
hairs grow limp, and the whole flower bends over. The
flies now walk out, covered with pollen, which they
promptly carry to another Dutchman's-pipe.

If you ever have a chance to see an open arum lily or
Dutchman's-pipe, you can probably find flies and other
tiny insects, hundreds of them, trapped inside. Both of

these unusual plants trap insects, keep them prisoner for a few days while the insects do the job of pollination, and then let them go.

There are other plants, however, that trap insects and do not let them go. These are the fantastic carnivorous, or meat-eating, plants. They have a different kind of partnership with insects, one that is quite one-sided. The insects, mainly small flies, provide food for the plants. The plants, instead of giving nectar or pollen, serve only as death traps for their insect visitors. Here are some of the best known of the insect-trapping plants that grow in our country.

VENUS'S-FLYTRAP. This strange plant is found only in one area, the coastal plains of North Carolina and northern South Carolina. It is most common in the grasslands around the city of Wilmington. The plant spreads open, traplike leaves close to the ground, ready for any crawling or flying insects that happen its way. Each leaf is in two parts, like a small clam shell, with a hinge on one side. Around the edge is a fringe of sharp points. Inside the leaves are sensitive hairs that serve as triggers. If an insect crawls into an open leaf and touches one of the hairs, even for a second, the two leaf halves close quickly, trapping the insect inside. The leaf crushes the insect, and glands inside the leaf pour out chemicals that actually digest the insect's body. It may take as long as a week till the insect has been completely digested. Then the fly-trapping leaf opens up again, ready to catch another insect.

This is a most unusual thing for a plant to do. Green plants, as you know, use energy from sunlight to make their own food from the raw materials found in air, in water, and in the minerals that are dissolved in the soil.

Venus's-flytrap

Flytraps and other insect-eating plants also react chemically to the insects they catch and to meat from other sources. The reason for this strange plant behavior is not clearly known. The use of insects by such plants is part of their adaptation to the particular environment in which they grow.

It is easy to raise Venus's-flytraps at home. Order live plants from one of the science supply companies listed on page 147. Plant them in garden soil in a flowerpot and keep them well watered. You will see the fly-trapping leaves grow and can test their trigger system by touching the inside of a leaf with a toothpick. You can also drop a small ant or even a tiny bit of raw meat onto an open leaf and see it snap shut and stay that way as the meat is digested. While the plants are called flytraps, it is known that they catch many kinds of small insects, especially beetles and ants, as well as flies. Seeing one of these plants at work will give you a view of a strange relationship between plants and insects.

SUNDEW. This is probably the most common and most widespread of all the carnivorous plants. It is a very tiny plant, and so it is often unnoticed even though it grows in bogs and marshes all over the world. In the United States, sundew plants can be found in damp places anywhere except in the Southwest.

The tiny sundew grows close to the ground, forming a little rosette of leaves, each smaller than a dime. The

top surface of each leaf is covered with tiny hairs tipped
with drops of sticky fluid. When sunlight falls on a sundew, its leaves glitter like diamond-studded jewels.
When a gnat or other tiny fly touches one of the spark-
ling leaves, it is hopelessly trapped. Its feet are held by
the sticky drops, and as it struggles to free itself, its wings
and body, too, are caught. The leaf acts like flypaper.
The more the insect thrashes around, the more tangled
and helpless it becomes. While the insect is trying to
free itself, the leaf hairs bend slowly toward the center,
enfolding the victim in a final death grip. Glands on the

Sundew

leaf then begin to pour juices over the insect, digesting it slowly.

Look for the tiny sundew plants if you are ever hiking in a marshy place. If you find one, dig it up carefully, with plenty of soil. Plant it in a coffee can or flowerpot when you get home and cover it with a glass or a clear plastic jar. This will make a little greenhouse for your sundew, where it will stay damp. Then you can experiment with the tiny leaves, feeding them gnats, the tiny flies that hover around ripe fruit, small ants, or pieces of meat as big as the head of a pin. Also, try using a tiny bit of wood, a grain of sand, or a bit of paper. You will find out that the sensitive hairs will clasp around the non-meat for a few moments and then let go. It is chemical as well as mechanical action that makes the leaf hairs hold onto a bit of meat.

PITCHER PLANTS. Other American carnivorous plants are those of the pitcher-plant family. All of them have round hollow leaves that stand up straight like pitchers. Three kinds of pitcher plants grow in three different parts of the country. The common Northern pitcher is found east of the Rocky Mountains, from Canada all the way south to Florida. The yellow-flowered pitcher plant grows in most of the Southern states, and the hooded pitcher, called the cobra plant, grows in California. Look for the pitcher plants along the edges of swamps and in other wet, marshy places.

The leaves of pitcher plants are like flowers in many ways. They are often colored with purple or red markings on a green or yellow background. They are round and open like many flower tubes and have nectar glands that produce a thick liquid that smells like ripe fruit. The leaves do not, however, contain any seed-making

Pitcher plant

parts. Like other carnivorous plants, pitcher plants have true flowers where the seeds are formed. The flower-like leaves serve mainly to lure insects and to digest them.

When a gnat lands on the open pitcher, it is led down the tube by small hairs, all pointing downward. Before it knows what is happening, the insect slides down to the bottom of the pitcher and into a pool of rain water and liquid chemicals made by the plant. Among the chemicals is one known to be a powerful killer. This chemical quiets the insects — gives it a kind of anesthetic — before it is digested.

If you cut open a leaf of a pitcher plant, you will find a rich, smelly insect soup filling the bottom of the pitcher. There will be dozens of tiny flies floating around, and usually parts of many dozen more. Any gnat or other small insect that walks, slides, or falls in has little or no chance of getting out of this pool of death.

When you observe the relationship between carnivorous plants and the insects that are trapped by them, you are seeing a partnership in which only one of the partners benefits. The insect, lured to the plant by scent or sight, is caught, held captive, killed, and absorbed chemically. The plant alone profits from such a partnership.

How fortunate for us that most of the insect-plant partnerships work out differently! Flowers provide food for the nectar-feeders, and the insects aid the flowers in their special job of making seeds. Insects and flowers, living together, keep the earth filled with a great variety of green plants, brilliant blossoms, luscious fruits, and useful seeds. It is a most efficient relationship, one in which each partner has become well adapted to the other through the years. It is a partnership that works well for them and fortunately also for us and is one that is likely to continue for many millions of years to come.

APPENDIXES

Appendix

A

SOME SCIENCES OF PLANTS AND INSECTS

If you are very much interested in plants and insects, you may want to study more about them as you go along in school. Science courses in high school and college will give you a background and many chances to do laboratory experiments. Some day you may want to consider a career in one of the sciences that deal with plants or insects.

BIOLOGY is the science of all living things. It is concerned with both plants and animals: the ways in which they grow and reproduce, their different parts and the functions of each part, and their dependence upon each other. It is also concerned with classification—the groups to which different living things belong. Scientists who work in biology are called biologists.

BOTANY is the science of all kinds of plants. It is a study of how plants are classified, how they are constructed, and how and where they grow. Botany, then, is really half of the study of biology. A scientist who works in the field of botany is a botanist.

ZOOLOGY is the other half of the science of biology. It is the study of animals: their kinds, the way they live, their environment, their various parts, and the way in which each part works. A scientist who works in this field is a zoologist.

ENTOMOLOGY is really a special branch of the study of zoology. It is concerned with insects: the many kinds, the way they live, their environment, their parts and the way each part works, their life cycles, and the relation of insects to man and other animals. A scientist who works in the field of entomology is an entomologist.

Whether or not you have used the names of the sciences before, you have discovered some important things in the fields of biology, botany, zoology, and entomology while you have been observing and investigating insects and plants and their amazing partnerships.

Appendix

B

WHERE TO BUY LIVE SPECIMENS

Insect eggs, cocoons, and chrysalises; bees and observation hives; and carnivorous plants:

Carolina Biological Supply Co.
Elton College, North Carolina

General Biological Supply House
8200 South Hoyne Avenue
Chicago 20, Illinois

New York Scientific Supply Co.
28 West 30th Street
New York 1, New York

Quivira Specialties Co.
4204 West 21st Street
Topeka, Kansas

Wards Natural Science Establishment
P.O. Box 1712
Rochester 3, New York

Wards of California
P.O. Box 1749
Monterey, California

Bees, observation hives, and information on bee hobbies:

A. I. Root Co.
Medina, Ohio

Carnivorous plants:

Clinton Nursery Products, Inc.
Boston Post Road
Clinton, Connecticut

Armstrong Associates, Inc.
Box 127
Basking Ridge, New Jersey

INDEX

Activities
  instructions for dissecting
    a pistil, 27-28
  instructions for experiment-
    ing with carnivorous
    plants, 137-141
  instructions for experiment-
    ing with stigma of a
    mimulus flower, 95
  instructions for finding
    nectar guides, 50-54
  instructions for investigating
    changes in grains of
    pollen, 28
  instructions for investigating
    flowers, 21-31, 88-89
  instructions for investigating
    insects, 33-36, 42-46, 71,
    78-80, 83, 103-106, 109-110
  instructions for investigating
    moths and butterflies, 46,
    103-106, 109-112, 116-118
  instructions for observing
    bees, 42-44, 78-80, 86-87
  instructions for observing
    beetles, 40-41, 71

instructions for observing
    honey making, 83
  instructions for observing
    wasps, 44
Alfalfa, 97-98
Anthers, 23-26
Avocado, 91-92

Barberry, 92-93
Bees
  bumblebees, 14, 83-84, 95-97,
    98-100
  characteristics of, 42-44,
    73-74
  feeding of, 42, 73-75, 113-114
  flower constancy of, 15,
    87-88, 114
  honey of, 80-83
  honeybees, 73-84
  instructions for observing,
    42-44, 78-80, 86-87
  instructions for observing
    honey making of, 83
  kinds of, 14, 74-76, 83-84,
    101-102
  life cycle of, 76-78

life in bee hive, 73-78, 83
mating of, 77
order of, 39-40, 42-44
partnership of red clover
    and bumblebees, 98-100
partnership of vanilla plant
    and stingless bee, 100-102
partnership with flowers, 73,
    78, 84, 85-86, 90-102
parts of, 78-81
pollination by, 85-86, 87-88,
    90-102
senses of, 86-87
swarming of, 76-78
Beetles
characteristics of, 40-41, 71
feeding of, 67-68, 70-72,
    113-114
fossils of, 66-67, 71-72
instructions for observing,
    40-41, 71
kinds of, 68-69
partnership of spicebushes
    and beetles, 68-70
partnership with flowers,
    67-72
pollination by, 67-72
senses of, 67-70
Biology, 145, 146
Botany, 145, 146
Buddleia (butterfly bush),
    103-104
Butterflies
characteristics of, 13, 44-46

feeding of, 45-46, 103-107,
    114
flower constancy of, 114
instructions for investigat-
    ing, 45-46, 103-106, 116-118
kinds of, 116-117
life cycle of, 114-118
partnership with flowers,
    103, 107-108, 114
parts of, 103-105
pollination by, 107-108, 114
senses of, 103-107

Coleoptera; see Beetles

Darwin, Charles, 48-49
Diptera; see Flies

Entomology, 146
Evolution
results of, 49-50, 65-67, 71-72,
    137
theory of, 48-49

Figs
fruit of, 58-60, 63-64
partnership with
    Blastophaga wasp, 59-64
pollination of, 58-64
Flies
characteristics of, 13, 41-42,
    128-130
partnership with flowers,
    128-141

partnership with fly-
    trapping plants, 131-141
pollination by, 129-135
Florets, 26-27, 99-100
Flowers
    bee, 85-102
    beetle, 67-71
    butterfly, 103, 107-108
    characteristics of, 15-19
    evolution of, 47-50, 65-68,
        71-72
    fly-trapping, 131-141
    grass, 30-31
    instructions for investigat-
        ing, 21-31, 88-89
    nectar of, 18-19
    nectar guides of, 16, 31-32,
        50-54, 67-69, 103, 107,
        111-113, 132-133, 140-141
    origin of, 65-67
    partnership with bees, 73,
        78, 84, 85-88, 90-102
    partnership with beetles,
        67-72
    partnership with butterflies,
        103, 107-108, 114
    partnership with flies,
        128-141
    partnership with insects,
        17-20, 47, 58-64, 67-72, 84,
        85-88, 90-102, 113, 114,
        119-127, 128-129, 130-142
    partnership with moths,
        113-114, 119-127

partnership with wasps,
    59-64
parts of, 22-28, 89, 107-108
pollen of, 22-24, 30-31, 68-69,
    88-89, 121-123, 132-134
pollination of, 27-32, 55-64,
    68-72, 84-85, 88, 90-102,
    107-108, 113-114, 121-123,
    129-135
stories of, 90-102, 119-127

Homoptera, 39-40
Honey, 80-83
Hymenoptera; *see* Bees, Wasps

Insects
    characteristics of, 12-15, 33,
        36-39
    evolution of, 48-50, 71-72
    fossils of, 66-67, 71-72
    instructions for investigat-
        ing, 33-36, 42-46, 71, 78-80,
        83, 103-106, 109-110
    nectar-feeding, 18-19, 31-32,
        33-46
    orders of, 39-46
    partnership with flowers, 17-
        20, 47, 58-64, 67-72, 84, 85-
        88, 90-102, 113, 114, 119-
        127, 128-129, 130-142 ˙
    parts of, 34-36, 78-81, 103-105
    pollination by, 31-32, 55-64,
        67-72, 85-86, 88, 90-102,

107-108, 113-114, 121-123,
129-135

Lepidoptera; *see* Moths,
        Butterflies

Mimulus (sticky monkey
        flower), 93-95
Moths
    characteristics of, 44-46,
        108-109
    flower constancy of, 114
    instructions for investigat-
        ing, 45-46, 109-112, 116-118
    kinds of, 117, 119-121
    life cycle of, 114-118, 123-127
    partnership with flowers,
        113-114, 119-127
    partnership with yucca
        plant, 119-127
    pollination by, 113-114, 119-
        120, 122-123, 126-127
    senses of, 109-113

Nectar
    as food for insects, 18-19, 31-
        32, 40-46, 67, 90-100, 105-
        107
    guides to, 16, 31-32, 50-54,
        67-69, 103, 107, 111-113,
        131-133, 140-141
    instructions for finding
        nectar guides, 50-54
    nectary for, 53-55, 70-71, 107

Ovary
    characteristics of, 25-28
    fertilization of, 27-29,
        121-124
Ovules; *see* Ovary

Partnership of insects and
        plants, 17-20, 58-64, 67-72,
        73, 84, 85-88, 90-102, 114,
        119-127, 128-129, 130-142
    beginning of, 65-67
    of caprifig and Blastophaga
        wasp, 59-64
    of fly-trapping plants and
        flies, 131-141
    of red clover and bumble-
        bees, 98-100
    of spicebushes and beetles,
        68-70
    of vanilla plant and stingless
        bee, 100-102
    of yucca and Pronuba moth,
        119-127
Pistil
    of butterfly flowers, 107-108
    characteristics of, 25-26,
        27-28
    instructions for dissecting,
        27-28
    of yucca flowers, 121-123
Pitcher plants, 139-141
Plants
    characteristics of, 47-50
    evolution of, 47-50, 65-68,
        71-72

Pollen
of bee flowers, 88-102
of beetle flowers, 68-70
characteristics of, 22-24
as food, 67, 71, 74-75, 78-79
of grass flowers, 30-31
importance in pollination,
28-31, 55-63, 68-69, 90-102,
121-124, 130-135
instructions for investigating
changes in grains of, 28
of yucca flowers, 121-124
Pollination
artificial, 102
by bees, 85-86, 87-88, 90-102
by beetles, 67-72
by butterflies, 107-108, 114
cross-, 28-32, 55-63, 90-102,
107-108, 121-123, 129-135
by flies, 129-135
by moths, 113-114, 119-120,
122-123, 126-127
process of, 28-32, 88
self-, 28-29, 55, 97-98
by wasps, 59-64
by wind, 30-31
Pussy willow, 90-91

Red clover, 98-100

Scotch broom, 95-97
Stamens
description of, 23-26, 107-108
importance in pollination,
28-31, 55-58, 68-69, 90-98,
107-108, 121-124, 130-135
Stigma
description of, 25-27
importance in pollination,
28-31, 55-57, 68-69, 90-102,
107-108, 113-114, 121-124,
130-135
instructions for experiment-
ing with stigma of mimu-
lus flower, 95
Sundew, 137-139

Vanilla, 100-102
Venus's flytrap, 135-137

Wasps
characteristics of, 42-44
instructions for observing, 44
partnership of caprifig and
Blastophaga wasp, 59-64

Yucca, 119-127

Zoology, 145-146